To Mary, Siobhan and Helen for your continuing support (GM)

To my wife, Christine, for her unstinting support (IA)

Creating Lifelong Learners

Challenges for education in the 21st century

Creating Lifelong Learners
Published April 2008

International Baccalaureate
Peterson House, Malthouse Avenue, Cardiff Gate
Cardiff CF23 8GL, Wales, GB
UNITED KINGDOM

Phone: +44 29 2054 7777
Fax: +44 29 2054 7778

Website: http//www.ibo.org

The International Baccalaureate (IB) offers three high quality and challenging educational programmes for a worldwide community of schools, aiming to create a better, more peaceful world.

IB merchandise and publications can be purchased through the IB store at http//store.ibo.org. General ordering queries should be directed to the sales and marketing department in Cardiff.

Phone: +44 29 2054 7746
Fax: +44 29 2054 7779

E-mail: sales@ibo.org

British Library Cataloguing in Publication data.
A catalogue record for this book is available from the British Library.

ISBN: 978-1-906345-02-0

Cover and text design: John Dickinson (www.johnddesign.co.uk)

Typeset and illustrated by Prepress Projects Ltd, UK (www.prepress-projects.co.uk)

Printed and bound by Athenaeum Press, Gateshead, UK.

Item code GD176

CONTENTS

Introduction

Today, we live in an increasingly flatter world in which the pace of technological, social and economic change has never been greater. These changes provide the opportunities for us to challenge many of the assumptions we may have about learning. We can now explore individual learning styles, examine brain-based learning approaches and consider the development of thinking skills, in addition to the implications of healthy living on the development of lifelong learning attitudes.

In the opening and closing sentences of its mission statement the IB sets clear challenges to all those who lead, teach and learn in those schools following the IB programmes:

> *The International Baccalaureate aims to develop inquiring, knowledgeable and caring young people who help to create a better and more peaceful world through intercultural understanding and respect.*
>
> *… These programmes encourage students across the world to become active, compassionate and lifelong learners who understand that other people, with their differences, can also be right.*

These aims are further clarified in the details of the IB learner profile (see Appendix):

> *The learner profile provides a long-term vision of education. It is a set of ideals that can inspire, motivate and focus the work of schools and teachers, uniting them in a common purpose.*

In the light of these IB challenges the aim of this book is to make a contribution to support school leaders and teachers at all levels as they strive to help encourage their students across the world to become active, compassionate and lifelong learners.

We hope this book helps by pointing to practical ways of challenging some assumptions and placing learning at the heart of school activities. In order to meet the challenges we need to ensure that teachers also are developed as knowledgeable inquirers, thinkers, communicators and above all remain open-minded risk takers able to reflect confidently on their lifelong learning journey.

> *If teachers never let their students see them as being learners, but only as knowers they are depriving the students of vital vicarious experience. Helping young people become better learners may mean daring to give up the belief that a teacher's top responsibility is to be omniscient.*
>
> Professor Guy Claxton (1999)

> *Our students have changed radically. Today's students are no longer the people our education system was designed to teach.*
>
> Marc Prensky (2001)

> *What if we set aside all discussion of things as they were, as they are and as they might become and concentrated on what they ought to be?*
>
> Dee Hock (1999)

Whether prompted by logical argument, visual representation, leading questions or examples of good practice, we hope that you enjoy exploring further just a small number of the fascinating challenges of learning that we now face, and that you use the opportunities to reflect on your contribution to developing high-quality learning for all our young people.

How to use this book

This book is designed to examine some of the strategies for developing approaches to learning. It does so by exploring theoretical background, offering practical implementation strategies, providing case studies of learning in practice and proposing challenges and possible solutions for school leaders. Therefore, this publication includes the following features:

Key questions

Key questions and challenges for school leaders, teachers and students—exploring how your organization is structured to deal effectively with change and how the culture of learning is developed.

Reflection

Moments of reflection/self-review for leaders, teachers and students—an opportunity too often ignored in our busy school lives. Here the focus is on your current personal position and how your experience and reflection impacts on those around you.

Strategies

A series of practical strategies or activities to be adapted for your own school organization—how the personal experience and culture may be developed through practice.

CASE STUDIES

Examples of case studies illustrating effective implementation, lessons learned through adopting a range of approaches to challenge assumptions about learning and the development of an open-minded approach to innovation.

Please use this publication according to your own particular learning style. You may wish to read through from cover to cover or dip in and out to focus on those strategies most relevant to help stimulate discussion in your school. You might seek to focus on practical activities that may be adapted to meet the needs of some of your learners, or to explore how particular case studies may be adapted to your own school.

We hope that this publication contributes to the ongoing debate about learning processes in a changing world and is taken in the spirit of the IB aim:

that other people, with their differences, can also be right.

CHAPTER 1

Developing learners in a changing world

Change is a constant factor in human history. What is distinctive now is the rate and scale of change.

(Robinson 2001)

In the early 1990s Dryden and Vos (2001), in their seminal work *The Learning Revolution*, wrote that:

For the first time in history, almost anything is possible.

Now, as we stand in the second half of the first decade of the 21st century, the statement of Dryden and Vos is perhaps more pertinent than ever. Through rapidly developing technology, programmes of research around the world and increasing opportunities to share best practices across continents, we are now able to apply greater knowledge and insight to the challenge of developing knowledgeable, caring young people with a love of learning for life.

To enable us to develop our knowledge we need to increase our awareness of the rapidly changing world in which our young people are growing up, and to approach with an open mind the growing range of strategies to help us meet the individual learning needs of our young people. An open mind is essential if we are to develop the best environment for lifelong learning.

The 21st-century learning experience

Before we briefly take note of the changing context in which our 21st-century students live and learn, let us first explore how that world impacts upon our own lives. In an increasingly fast-paced, digital world reflection and stillness is often a lost learning art. In light of this, why not spend a few moments in personal reflection on your lifelong learning journey to this point?

Reflection

Reflection

How many different career paths have you followed?

At what age did you become a teacher?

When you were 12 years old, how many TV channels did you have to choose from?

Did you use a computer as a student?

When did you first use e-mail?

What was the predominant teaching method when you were a student?

We should also consider some fundamental organizational questions.

Key questions

Can we clearly articulate the main purposes of schooling in the 21st century?

Do those purposes vary from nation to nation and learner to learner, or do they remain fundamentally constant?

How aware is your organization of how research and experience can help bring about high-quality, relevant learning?

Do the ways in which we currently organize our schools help or hinder high-quality, 21st-century learning?

Who are our schools designed and built for?

Do we wish to continue to develop high-quality learning incrementally, or to transform the experiences of our schools?

The pace of change

In 2001 Marc Prensky wrote about digital natives being taught by digital immigrants, and commented:

> *Our students have changed radically. Today's students are no longer the people our educational system was designed to teach.*

In light of your personal reflection and approach to the key questions you may be able to place yourself on a continuum of digital immigrants to digital natives, that is those of us who may feel uncomfortable with or even antagonistic towards the inexorable march of new technologies that increasingly define our everyday lives and educational experiences through to those, largely our students, who embrace the instant communication, personalized media and virtual worlds of today. By exploring our own perceptions and those of our colleagues and students we may begin to appreciate and question where we stand in the rapidly flowing river of 21st-century living and learning. When so many leading educational and social thinkers have commented on the times we now live in as the fastest changing in mankind's history it is perhaps pertinent to reflect on the impact of this pace of change on ourselves and our organizations.

Today's students have been brought up in an interactive world—recent research indicates that typical teenagers are likely to study with five or more software programs open on their laptop computer, while they listen to their digital personal music player, with a television providing a background to their activities. As Prensky (2001) says:

> *Today's students think and process information fundamentally differently from their predecessors.*

Do you:

Print off most of your emails?

Phone to ask if someone received your email?

Know how many pages are available on Google?

Call someone in to show them a website?

Work on no more than two programs at any one time?

Know how fast the World Wide Web is growing?

Remember when floppy disks really were floppy?

As leaders in schools, whether as head teachers, programme managers or classroom teachers, we are likely to have employed quite different methods of study and our social situations probably varied greatly from those of our students growing up in the late 20th and early 21st centuries.

Young people today are much more likely to parallel process and multitask, to use instant messaging and work in networks, to expect to receive information very quickly, and to prefer instant gratification and constant praise. On the other hand, their teachers are more likely to have achieved in their lives through logical step-by-step approaches to learning, in which all members of their group were taught at the same pace.

John Dewey (1916), an American philosopher and educational reformer, wrote:

> *If we teach today as we taught yesterday, we rob our students of tomorrow.*

Never have these words seemed so relevant—and yet they were written in 1916 in his book *Democracy and Education*, which stresses the importance of active cooperative learning.

To achieve some perspective on the pace of change today it is interesting to explore some of the extraordinary facts that illustrate those areas impacting upon the learning world of our young people.

Let us begin with a small test of your knowledge. How much do you know of the following: Dongguan, Dalian, Sialkot? Answers later.

Do you recognize this figure?

340,282,366,920,938,000,000,000,000,000,000,000,000

The above figure, created by IPv6, the new Internet protocol, will be the number of Internet addresses that will be made available over the next year. It is needed because by 2009 all of the 4 billion addresses currently available will have been used up.

In 2006, 50 billion emails were dispatched each day—a four-fold increase on 2001. And yet it was only in 1993 that Marc Andreessen, an American student earning only US$6 an hour, created the first Internet browser—Netscape Navigator.

Information on the Web doubles every 90 days. The Web has 140 new first-time users a minute: almost 75 million a year. One hundred and fifty medical research papers are published on the Web each day, and the popular search engine Google processes 1 billion Web searches a day.

In late 2007, the number of text messages sent in one day was greater than the population of our planet.

The above pace of change means that:

▶ Undergraduates may access more information in one year than both their grandparents would have accessed in a lifetime.

Key questions

How do you see the impact of the digital age touching the lives of your students?

In an information age, what additional skills do we need to teach our students?

What are the implications of the World Wide Web for our methodologies of assessment?

How can we respond to the question "if we do not know what the future may look like, how can we prepare our students?"

How, as facilitators of learning, do we engage our young people?

What key values do we expect of the global citizens of the 21st century?

▶ Four out of five children starting school this year are likely to enter careers that do not yet exist, using technology that has not yet been invented.

▶ Employees will change professions, not just jobs, four or five times in their working life.

A flatter world

It is clear that we live in an age of instant communication in which knowledge is available at the click of a mouse. This is revolutionizing the way in which we work, learn, shop and are entertained.

In order to prepare our young people to learn more effectively, it is important to note the impact of the digital information revolution on the world they share as global citizens.

In his 2005 book *The World is Flat*, Thomas L Friedman notes:

> *Clearly it is now possible for more people than ever to collaborate and compete in real time with more other people on more different kinds of work from more different corners of the planet and on a more equal footing than at any previous time in the history of the world.*

Friedman examines the impact of new globalization on the developing career opportunities of our global citizens. With the rapid development of outsourcing of design, manufacturing and servicing to China, India, eastern Europe and South America, our world is becoming smaller and flatter.

A consultant in London may have the analysis of an brain scan provided overnight by technicians in India or Australia. A New York accountant may have a significant amount of work undertaken by accountancy graduates in India. Similarly, there have been significant developments in IT outsourcing, notably to Brazil and China. There are over 2 million software designers in China, a number increased by "Sea Turtles", or US-educated business and IT experts returning to their home country. Significant IT investment in Brazil (with proximity to the USA and its time zones, and with a state of the art telecommunications infrastructure) has led to the country's banking system being one of the most automated in the world and it is attracting outsourcing investment at a rapidly increasing rate. Thus, the working lives of global citizens have changed at an astonishingly rapid rate—with the roles of individuals and their ability to link to others creating new opportunities and changing the world in perhaps the most profound manner we have ever experienced.

As Friedman (2005) points out:

> *This flattening process is happening at warp speed and directly or indirectly touching a lot more people on the planet at once ... and that is why the great challenge for our time will be to absorb these changes in ways that do not leave them behind.*

The implications for educational change in the 21st century are represented by the Imaginaries of David Hargreaves (2004) (Figure 1.1).

19th-century Imaginary	vs.	21st-century Imaginary
Learning is the acquisition of curriculum content		Learning includes how to learn
Roles are sharply defined and segregated		Roles are blurred and overlapped

Figure 1.1: Imaginaries of David Hargreaves

Hargreaves (2004) points us to an increasingly personalized approach to learning—how to learn, rather than the acquisition of parcels of knowledge. As Toffler (1970) states:

> *The illiterate of the year 2000 will not be the individual who cannot read and write, but the one who cannot learn, unlearn and relearn.*

This theme of the rapidity of world change and its implications for our global learners is further explored in Daniel H Pink's (2005) book, *A Whole New Mind*, in which he poses the view that:

> *In an increasingly flat, global, information-rich world we need to ensure we develop the 'right-brain' qualities of creativity, inventiveness, empathy and joyfulness.*

We will explore these concepts, and how an understanding of how our brain works influences our learning, in Chapter 2.

And what of Dongguan, Dalian and Sialkot?

Dongguan is now the third largest exporting city in mainland China, with 15,000 international companies based there and a population that has risen from 1 million in the 1970s to over 7 million today. It is a city where approximately 40% of the world's computer parts are produced.

Dalian is the Silicon Valley of north-east China, with 22 colleges and universities and over 200,000 students, and is the city where Japanese companies have now invested in the research and development of software.

Sialkot, in Pakistan, is where 85% of the world's footballs are made.

These are just three examples of a rapidly changing world that requires new skills from our teachers and learners. They are indicative of a shifting global economy that, more than ever, challenges educators to ensure true global understanding, cultural awareness and flexibility of individualized learning to engage, motivate and prepare our young people for their new world.

Individual learning in the new age

A recent survey for the Bill and Melinda Gates Foundation in the United States, "The Silent Epidemic, Perspectives of High School Dropouts" (Bridgeland *et al.* 2006) pointed out that:

> most dropouts are students who could have, and believe they could have succeeded in school ... the general reasons they fail remain constant—a lack of connection to the school environment; a perception that school is boring; feeling unmotivated; academic challenges and the weight of real world events.

Thus, as Prensky (2001) also points out, teachers may recognize these types of students:

- ▶ those who are truly self-motivated
- ▶ those who are going through the motions
- ▶ those who believe that what they are being taught is of little relevance to their lives but also realize that they need their qualifications for the future
- ▶ those students who increasingly "tune out" or lose interest, convinced that school is devoid of relevance to their lives.

Prensky (2001) sees that teachers who are assisting those students to learn are faced with a challenge—"engage me or enrage me". In our digital world, our young people increasingly have the opportunity to be engaged. They are able to select and edit their personal world of music, converse with peers around the world, view multiple television channels and access billions of pages of information from their bedrooms.

This change in communication access and blurring of boundaries requires newer approaches to individualized learning.

CASE STUDY

Kariman Mango/History teacher/Ahliyyah School for Girls/Amman, Jordan

Learning through history

The history department aims to move students away from the traditional view of history as a set of facts to be learned and memorized. We want our students to understand the nature of history, and the problems of historical interpretation and its significance. The focus of classes is on historical analysis in the hope that students will appreciate the relevance of history to their everyday lives while enhancing their critical thinking skills.

Debates and role-playing are used throughout the courses to engage students with different learning styles and to create more independent learners.

Students in Grade 10 put Hitler on trial and decide on whether he was most to blame for the outbreak of the second world war.

Structured class debates on who was most to blame for the cold war allow students to research their arguments and participate in a debate; this is followed up with student essays.

Orchestrated immersion

Based on the idea that the human brain learns through experience, orchestrated immersion is an attempt to immerse students in learning through appealing to their senses. Islamic history students, for example, have to cover the once-great Ottoman dynasty, including units on the art and architecture of Islam. They learn all this through their texts and classes. But to truly bring the topics to life, visits to locations of importance in the Islamic past are organized every year in order to immerse students in the experience. The school and teachers provide the students with an orchestrated learning experience; students interact with the subject in a more physical and concrete manner. The trip allows for a visualization of the past.

The IB Islamic history field trip usually takes place early on in the academic year in Grade 11; later on in the course, students are expected to work on internal assessment research projects, when they are encouraged to make connections between their experience on the field trip and their internal assessment. Students are expected to do something with their experience.

The field trip also doubles as a visual arts experience, and students are expected to use their experience in their visual arts work—as seen below in the example of wall charts.

Wall charts

Students produce a variety of wall charts, which can technically be used for any subject. Instead of the teacher following the traditional method of providing students with information, the students are set a task.

For example, Grade 11 Islamic history students are expected to understand the nature of the Arabs in pre-Islamic Arabia. Students are divided up into small groups and each group is provided with certain aspects of the life of the Arabs in pre-Islamic Arabia, for example the origin of the Arabs, religion in pre-Islamic Arabia, the importance of genealogy to the pre-Islamic Arabs, poetry in pre-Islamic Arabia, etc.

Students are assigned reading material, from which they are expected to extract the relevant information. They are expected to produce a wall chart clarifying their assigned topics.

Students are told beforehand what the assessment criteria are, and they are provided with a rubric highlighting what areas will be assessed and what marks will be assigned to each section. Students are assessed on knowledge and accuracy, visual representation, originality and creativity.

Students then present their charts to the class and a question and answer session follows.

Students are, however, given the option of creating booklets or PowerPoint® presentations instead of wall charts.

Timelines

Another method used to help students conceptualize history is the creation of timeline wall charts. This activity is usually more suited to the lower grades and is a perfect way to introduce younger students to the concept of chronology. It can, however, be used with older students, especially when very large timeframes are being used.

As an introductory activity, students in Grade 11 Islamic history create an annotated timeline of Islamic history, from the birth of the prophet Muhammad in 570 to the collapse of the Ottoman Empire in 1924. Students this year were provided with timeline sheets and reading material, and were then expected to annotate their timelines with the main dynasties and their ruling periods. The ideal scenario for such a timeline would be to create one on a classroom wall, using coloured paper. This would visually represent a large block of time, and the timeline would also be around as a visual reference for the rest of the year.

The challenge is to continue to engage our students by increasing our awareness and understanding of the world they inhabit and by developing our knowledge, understanding and application of an increasing range of individual learning strategies to engage, motivate and inspire our students—"to create a better world through education".

Reflecting on our learning

Perhaps one aspect of our roles that we must ensure is not ignored is that of reflection or metacognition—thinking about our learning and thinking about our thinking. We should not lose sight of the fundamental elements of the learning process—the encouragement of curiosity and unlocking of interest through challenge and inspiration and creating the environment to draw learning out of our students.

Combes *et al.* (1994), for example, define the process as follows:

Learning always consists of two parts: first, confrontation with new information or experience; second, discovery of personal, individual meaning.

Therefore, how, as teachers, might we react to the following possible questions from our students?

Key questions

Why am I taught at the speed of other students?

Why am I forced to fail exams this year when I could pass them next?

Why do I learn a foreign language alongside others who can't use it?

Why do I have to memorize information I can look up on my mobile phone?

Why are there so few subjects when there are hundreds of TV channels?

Why do I have to write in school when everyone types in life?

Why is school analogue and grey when life is digital and technicolour?

By reflecting on the above questions we can further consider how to ensure that our school's learning culture is truly global, relevant to our students' individual needs and inculcates a lifelong love of learning.

A uniform way of teaching and testing is patently unsatisfactory when everyone is so different.

(Gardner 1993)

In thinking about our own learning experience and that of our students, we must consider whether we organize our structures, processes and teaching to ensure that each individual leaves us having enjoyed learning, being encouraged to continue learning in the future, and remaining interested and involved (perhaps the two key factors leading to success in the future). The development of wider skills than memorizing and reporting facts is increasingly important—with a greater focus on problem-solving, team-building and empathy needed in our flatter world of shared learning.

CASE STUDY

KARIMAN MANGO/HISTORY TEACHER/AHLIYYAH SCHOOL FOR GIRLS/AMMAN, JORDAN

Practical simulations

The idea behind these practical simulations is that history should not be taught as a series of facts that students must digest and then reproduce later on. History is not about when something happens; it is about why something happens. Students are encouraged to foster historical empathy; they are encouraged to understand why certain individuals in history acted in the manner they did by putting themselves in their shoes. Instead of giving them sterile historical information, students are provided with scenarios and asked what they would do in that situation.

The Treaty of Versailles

Students take on the role of the Big Three at the Treaty of Versailles. They are provided with information on the characters and circumstances of each of the three leaders, and are then provided with a list of issues the leaders must decide on. Students are expected to make informed decisions based on what they know about their assigned leaders.

They are then expected to negotiate with the other two leaders and produce a treaty as a group. This gives them the chance to realize how difficult it is to come to a compromise in such a situation.

Students are assessed on their knowledge application, and teamwork and the accuracy of their final product.

They share their final treaty with the rest of the class and, after all groups have shared their information, the real terms of the treaty are introduced to the class and the actual treaty can be compared with their expected treaties.

The Cuban missile crisis

Students must imagine that they are advising President Kennedy on what possible options he had at the time of the Cuban missile crisis. They are provided with several options, ranging from carrying out a surgical air strike to using negotiation and diplomacy. Students are expected to work in groups and provide a list of pros and cons for each of the suggested actions; they are then expected to choose one course of action they feel the president should take.

The groups present to the class the course of action they feel would be most appropriate for the president to take; this usually sparks a class discussion as to the merits of the suggested action.

After all groups have presented, Kennedy's actual actions are introduced to students.

As Ken Robinson (2001) points out in his book *Out of Our Minds*:

> *There is an urgent need to rethink some of the underlying assumptions if we are seriously to tackle the development of creative resources in all our people. This is not just a matter of technical change: it means confronting deep-seated assumptions that underpin our view of ourselves and of each other, and the ways in which these are promoted through sustained years of formal education and training.*

We must also consider what schools should not be about—every student knowing the same things, having been prepared for remembering and regurgitating that information for one-off examinations, only to forget it as soon as they leave the room.

To achieve IB aims as school leaders and teachers, we have to ensure that we re-examine the culture, attitudes and methodology of learning in our schools and remain receptive, open-minded and critically aware of developments in our understanding of learning in a time of such rapid change. Over the next several chapters we explore some of those developments relating to the science of learning and the brain, emotional intelligence and engagement and the holistic approach to individualized learning.

> *In times of change, the learners will inherit the earth ... while the knowers will find themselves beautifully equipped to deal with a world that no longer exists.*
>
> *(Hoffer 1942)*

Chapter 2

The brain and learning development

A mind once stretched by a new idea can never go back to its original dimension.

(Holmes 1858)

So we live in an age of exponential change, as new technology and instant communication feeds our knowledge society. In our world of learning this is particularly exemplified by the rapid developments in the understanding of how the brain operates. We also live at a time of confluence: when new technology, in the form of non-invasive imaging systems in neuroscience, meets the tributaries of psychology of learning and emotional intelligence to create a flow of knowledge towards the holy grail of how we best learn.

In a book that deals with 21st-century learning it is imperative that we examine how this developing of an understanding of the brain impacts upon learning. However, we also need to acknowledge that such a vast topic lends itself to a whole series of books. With limited space we can only hope to stimulate interest for further research and point to some of the key areas of understanding to assist in meeting the IB learner profile objective of developing motivated, self-aware, lifelong learners. The following quotations from three leading experts in the field of neuroscience highlight the extent of the challenge facing those exploring how the brain works.

In 1997 Professor Susan Greenfield acknowledged:

The brain still remains a tantalising mystery to those of us who have been studying it for most of our lives; it often seems that the more we learn the more there is still to learn.

While, in 2003, Professor Richard Restak noted:

Twenty-first century discoveries about the brain will provide us with new insights into our behavioural thinking and feelings. Thanks to technological advances, neuroscientists are already successfully correlating brain function with personality.

In 2006 Professor Elkhonon Goldberg wrote:

> *While perusing any standard text you are not likely to encounter*
> *any reference to the gender differences in brain organisation,*
> *let alone to individual difference. But such differences do exist*
> *and we are only now beginning to understand them. From the*
> *aerial view of all humanity represented by a composite, we are*
> *gradually moving to the understanding of the neural foundations of*
> *individuality.*

As research continues to develop our understanding of the brain through powerful new imaging technologies, so the quest continues to establish the extent to which our brain impacts on how we learn. An understanding of the brain and its influence on learning should be seen as a crucial part of the true implementation of the IB learner profile as it sharpens "the focus for schools where it belongs: on learning" and will assist in the development of coherence across the IB through "ongoing professional development for our teachers". This focus on brain-based approaches to learning encourages the shift from whole-class teaching and the transmission of learning to the understanding of the uniqueness of each learner. This leads on to exploration of the psychology of learning and the importance of emotional intelligence, engagement and motivation in the unlocking of the learner as a genuine inquirer developing a lifelong enjoyment for learning.

As over 90% of what we now know about the brain and learning has developed through new technology and research over the past 10 to 20 years, there is clearly a need to develop our teachers as inquirers to explore the impact of "brain-based" learning approaches.

How the brain works

> *Our brain has always defined the education profession, yet*
> *educators haven't really understood it or paid much attention to it.*
> *(Sylwester 1995)*

The human brain is generally accepted to be one of the world's most complicated structures, with over 100 billion cells and an estimated power of at least 100 trillion connections. Our brain defines how we see and interpret the world around us and establishes our unique fingerprint of learning; yet this organ of individual definition looks remarkably similar in each of us. Weighing about 1400 g and consisting of 75–80% water, 10% fat and 8% protein, it has the appearance and consistency of a large piece of fungus. It makes up 2% of our body weight but it uses 20% of the body's energy as it processes several billion pieces of information every second.

> *While most educators are interested in how the mind works and what they can do to enhance learning, knowing how the brain itself works is an important prerequisite in shaping the brain-compatible classroom.*

> *(Fogarty 1997)*

Our understanding of the brain has developed over thousands of years, from around 500 BC with Alcmaeon's view of the brain as the centre of sensation, to Hippocrates, who referred to the brain's uniqueness, through to Galen in 130−200 AD who, as a physician to gladiators, noted the central importance of the brain to physical and mental abilities. In more modern times, due to animal research and anatomical study (with a diversion into phrenology in the early 19th century), through to the work of Purkinje, Cajal and Golgi in the late 19th and early 20th centuries, the foundations of our limited knowledge of the brain and how it works have been established.

These foundations have been built on by further research, such as that by Maclean. His triune brain view (Figure 2.1) shows a hierarchy: (i) the reptilian brain, the brain stem responsible for insinctive behaviour (freeze, fight or flight); (ii) the mammalian middle brain or limbic system, which controls emotional behaviour; (iii) the thalamus and hypothalamus, controlling the senses, and often referred to as the emotional gate to the intellect; and (iv) the cortex, or new mammalian outer layer, which houses the area for rational thoughts, a "bark" that constitutes 85% of the total brain. Contemporary opinions emphasize a more complex view whereby emotional functioning is seen to operate beyond the limbic system throughout the brain. Maclean does, however, help us in looking at the basic structure of the brain.

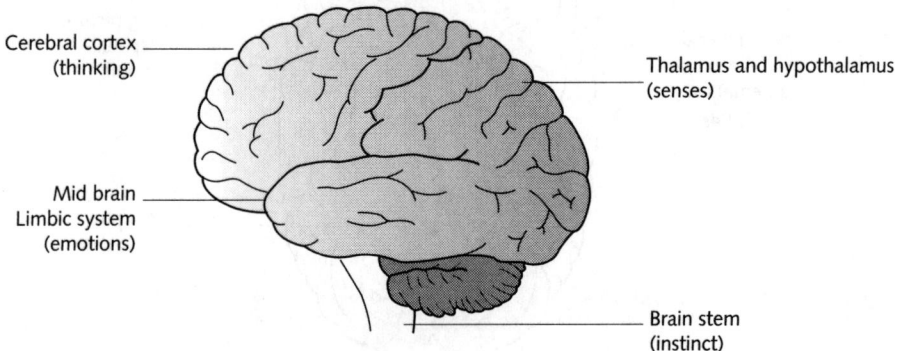

Figure 2.1: Basic structures of the brain

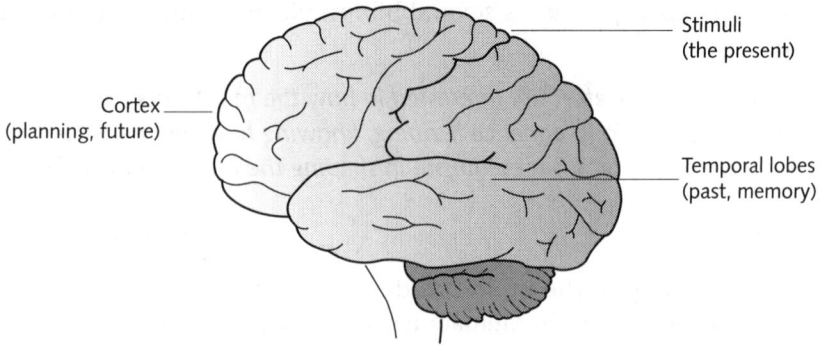

Figure 2.2: Front-to-back view of the brain

A further view of the geography of the brain may be made by looking front to back to identify particular functions (Figure 2.2). This view notes that the pre-frontal cortex focuses on planning (the future); the middle section is most sensitive to stimuli in the present; and the rear part of the brain, with the temporal lobes, deals with the organization of memories often stimulated through our senses.

Viewed from above, the brain is divided into two hemispheres, connected by the bridge of the corpus callosum. Each hemisphere deals with different tasks while communicating with the other (Figure 2.3). The general view is that each hemisphere has different processing purposes, with the left focusing on sequential, logical thought while the right focuses on spatial and visual thought and the overall "big picture". The different emphases and the way in which the brain develops its internal communication pathways do have clear implications for lifelong learning skills.

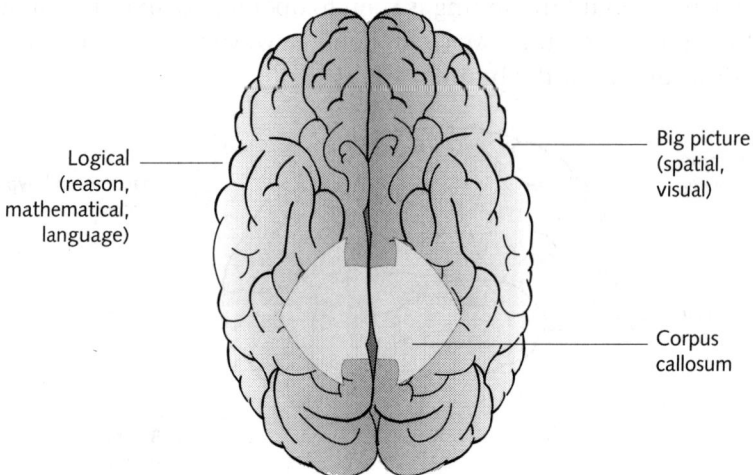

Figure 2.3: The brain viewed from above

Neurobiological research into how the brain operates has also developed rapidly in recent years due to advances in brain imaging technology. Through these non-invasive techniques we can now examine the functioning elements of the brain in operation. The brain is composed of neurons and glial cells, which form a layer of insulation, or myelin, around nerve fibres. In operation, messages are received by neurons as electrical impulses and conducted by axons, which then create chemical interaction between cells. The scale of these messages is difficult to conceptualize—as Professor Greenfield (1997) explains:

> *If you counted the connections between this outer layer at a rate of one connection a second it would take 32 million years . . . over four times longer than it has taken human beings to evolve.*

To understand this most complex organ, simple models are often proposed—most notably the view of the brain as a super-computer. Sylwester argues that this is inappropriate as it suggests that the brain is controlled by logic, programmed by an external force. Edelman's view of the brain as the layered ecology of a jungle environment is preferred, whereby the various interconnected organisms respond to environmental challenges.

> *Thus we have a modular brain, in that a relatively small number of standard non-thinking components combine their information to create an amazingly complex cognitive environment.*
>
> *(Sylwester 1995)*

So how would increasing our understanding of the brain, its structure and complex processes influence learning?

Reflection

As we learn more about the brain does it imply that we often underestimate the capacity of the learner?

Should we extend our learning to avoid reliance on generalizations and oversimplification of some brain-based learning approaches?

To what extent does our current facilitation of learning respect the unique nature of each learner?

Now, after research has developed in the late 20th and early 21st centuries, some of the principal areas of agreement are that:

- ▶ Multiple brain regions contribute to different functions.
- ▶ The brain's plasticity enables new neural networks to develop throughout life.
- ▶ Experience, learning and emotion strengthen and develop neural networks.
- ▶ Our senses stimulate brain action.

▶ More recent theories point to the innate nature of brain function—that is, the hard-wiring basic survival neural network.
▶ This hard-wiring is affected and the brain is developed through its environment.
▶ Both sides of the nature versus nurture debate may gain points of relevance from continuing brain research.

The above points are neatly summed up by Sylwester (1995):

> *Unfortunately biological evolution proceeds at a very much slower pace than cultural evolution so we're forced to grapple with current social and environmental issues using a brain that biological evolution has tuned to the far different cognitive challenge of 30,000 years ago.*

A renewed look at current strategies from a brain-based learning perspective can ensure increased teacher awareness of the individual nature of the learning process.

CASE STUDY

AHLIYYAH SCHOOL FOR GIRLS/AMMAN, JORDAN

Different strategies for learning

Various teaching and learning strategies used at ASG have been successful. These strategies could relate to the IB learner profile, brain-based learning approaches or particular methods used to deliver the programmes.

Whiteboards

In an effort to enhance teaching and learning at the ASG and in light of the knowledge that all learners learn differently, one of the new teaching strategies the school is currently involved in is the use of interactive whiteboards. The thinking behind the introduction of this type of technology is based on the idea that all of our students learn differently and the interactive whiteboard is one way of audiovisually enhancing the learning experience.

The boards, if used effectively, also allow lessons to become more student-centric. Students create and present work to the class on the interactive whiteboards. They also allow for the use of online lessons and resources.

Diverse forms of assessment

ASG has been involved in a concerted effort to move away from paper-and-pen style assessments. Student evaluation, becoming more project based, is moving away from exam-based assessment. Taking into account different learning styles means that different styles of assessment need to be introduced.

Group learning

Reorganizing classroom layout into group or cooperative learning models is one method we use to enhance the way our students learn and interact with each other and also the way in which our teachers teach.

To develop necessary lifelong learning skills in a time of exponential change it is important that we take note of the developing understanding of the brain and ensure that we relate that knowledge to learning processes, structures and environment. Clearly, we can enhance learning through stimulating the senses, by recognizing the uniqueness of each learner and by establishing effective rigour, challenge, pace and engagement.

To explore how we may do that, let's focus on one or two key aspects of the brain models.

Right and left hemispheres

Building on the work of Nobel Laureate Roger Sperry, concerning the functioning differences of the two hemispheres, researchers now note that both hemispheres are involved in nearly all human activity. There is general agreement that the left hemisphere processes sequentially in "parts" while the right processes "wholes". The left hemisphere, therefore, has responsibility for analytical processes, reason and deductions. The right, with more white than grey matter, has a greater focus on communicative aspects. Women do tend to have a proportionally larger corpus callosum, thus providing greater connections between the two hemispheres, lending credence to the opinion that women are better able to multi-task. It might also help to explain the emotional differences between men and women. Men tend to separate emotions in the two hemispheres, with the right focusing on negative and the left focusing on positive feelings. Men also tend to focus language processing in the left hemisphere and emotions in the right, perhaps explaining the view that they have a lower tendency to verbalize their emotions. Clearly, there are implications for the range of learning strategies to be used in the coeducational classroom.

An example of the left/right hemisphere differences can be obtained by closing your eyes for a few moments and then quickly opening them. What you will see first will be the general outlines of the scene. Then, as you focus on particular objects in contextual detail, the right hemisphere gives you the whole picture while the left enables you to analyse the scene in detail. Clearly, both hemispheres are generally required to enable us to make sense of the world. This may be seen as a metaphor for our learning process, whereby we use our left hemisphere to analyse and process to enable us to understand the ever-growing bigger picture. As Carl Sagan points out in *The Dragons of Eden*, there is no way to tell whether the patterns extracted by the right hemisphere are real or imagined without subjecting them to left hemisphere scrutiny. To solve complex problems in changing circumstances requires the activity of both cerebral hemispheres.

Key questions

To what extent do we take into account the differences between male and female students' language and emotional development?

Are we aware of our own left/right hemisphere preferences?

Are we aware of our students' preferences?

As teachers, are we sufficiently "brain aware"?

Does the range of classroom learning strategies reflect brain awareness?

Are our students "brain aware"?

Strategies

Possible approaches to enhance "whole-brain" learning may be:
- ▶ Give the picture first (RH) and then break down into parts (LH)
- ▶ Describe with words (L) or a diagram or picture (R)
- ▶ Visualize outcome (R) then describe it to another person (L)
- ▶ Use mind mapping (L & R)
- ▶ Use music (R)
- ▶ Make use of Brain Gym® (L & R)

Reflection

Do you have a tendency towards right or left hemisphere dominance in your learning preferences?

Quickly respond Y (Yes) or N (No) to the following statements:
   a   I constantly look at a clock or wear a watch.
   b   I find it hard to follow directions precisely.

    c I think it's easier to draw a map than tell someone how to get somewhere.

    d I frequently let my emotions guide me.

    e I learn maths with ease.

    f I'd read the instructions before assembling something.

    g People tell me I am always late getting places.

    h I need to set goals for myself to keep me on track.

    i I'd probably make a good detective.

    j I use a lot of gestures.

    k If someone asks me a question, I turn my head to the right.

    l I keep a "to do" list.

    m I am able to thoroughly explain my opinions in words.

    n I always lose track of time.

    o When I'm confused, I usually go with my gut instinct.

Answering "yes" to questions a, e, f, h, i, k, l and m indicates left hemisphere dominance whereas positive answers to questions b, c, d, g, j, n and o indicates right hemisphere dominance.

Key questions

How might our increasing brain awareness impact on learning processes?

How might left/right hemisphere preference influence learning?

How might our understanding of memory encourage a range of learning strategies?

The way the brain develops and the location of functions in the two hemispheres has relevance to our understanding of the learning process. We are, for example, born with the capacity to learn any of the world's 3,000+ languages with the hard-wired ability located in the left hemisphere. As we learn other languages later in life, it is via different processes focused in the right hemisphere—hence the value of early exposure to other languages.

Memory

Memory clearly plays a vital part in the development of the lifelong learner. John Ratey (2003) of Harvard Medical School described memory as:

> *The centripetal force which pulls together learning, understanding and consciousness—with the brain more like an active ecosystem than a static pre-programmed computer.*

We now understand that memories occur at the synapse through long-term potentiation: the storage of memory the instant it happens, when neurons are altered and create new patterns (which can take up to two days to happen). A longer-term memory tends to develop through emotional connection—we remember where we were when President Kennedy was assassinated or when the events of 9/11 were unfolding. This suggests implications for the role of memory in learning. Do we recall more easily and frequently those special events that stand out or those actions we have repeated rather than the mundane or passively received aspects of learning through transmission of knowledge? As Sylwester (1995) points out:

> It doesn't take much input to trigger a strong memory, but it takes a lot of mental activity to activate a weak memory ... [memory] is more adaptive and inventive and over time experience adds depth and breadth. Unfortunately much of our school testing programme requires our students' very inventive biological memory system to exhibit high-level technological precision.

The most recent research refers to two principal forms of memory: declarative (or explicit) memory and procedural (or implicit) memory. The latter may be seen as those series of skills we develop, such as driving a car or riding a bike, through repetition but also emotional memory, which is extremely powerful and may be linked to great joy or sadness. The former deals with names: knowledge that may be verbalized and also episodes or events. Each is located largely in a different area of the brain: declarative in the hippocampus and procedural in the amygdala.

An awareness by the learner of the different forms of memory might be used to deploy different strategies to develop the quality and effectiveness of memory. As Jensen and Johnson (1995) point out, "engage the emotions; make the learning personally compelling, deeply felt and real". This may be achieved through creative controversy, role plays, music, debates and celebrations—events that arouse feeling, which reinforces learning impact.

Recent research also reinforces the significance of the impact of our senses on the memory and how this may be strengthened through repetition, as Restak (2003) points out:

> If you want to learn a new skill or make use of new knowledge you must change your brain. You must engage in repetitive exercises that set up the relevant circuits and sharpen their expression.

Professor Richard Wiseman (2003) notes that:

> *We don't process verbal information anything like as efficiently as that received visually.*

If we add this to research indicating the need for adolescents particularly to have had access to extensive mobility when learning, we can see the implications for the development of a visually stimulating learning environment and the creation of opportunities to strengthen neural networks by adopting a range of kinaesthetic activities.

Memory helps understanding by establishing a context, selecting and connecting to form relevance, and reinforces knowledge and skills through the building of patterns—linking and strengthening those vital neural pathways. Many of the modern memory techniques that form part of an increasing range of commercial learning packages for businesses today are founded on those used in ancient times. We remember more by personalizing information, by making it emotionally relevant—thus selecting what is significant—exaggerating it, connecting it to a context and explaining it to others. This is an example of what Alistair Smith (2002) refers to as "Your Memory Specs"—See it, Personalize it, Exaggerate it, Connect it and Share it.

Key questions

How much learning in your classroom is based on visual and kinaesthetic approaches?

Do you ensure that important events are made special by introducing novel ways of monitoring and connecting material?

Are you aware of the different ways in which your learners remember?

Do you ensure there is a sufficient range of strategies to engage enquiry in your learners?

Implications for learning

Our principal aim has been to arouse interest in how the brain affects the learning experience. Having explored the development of brain knowledge, left/right hemispheres and how memory works, it seems appropriate at this point to refer to implications for the development of the learner, using the IB learner profile as a base.

An increased understanding of intellectual, personal, emotional and social growth can be enhanced by an understanding of the biological development of our brain. There is a need to move from the metaphor of the super-computer able to be programmed by inputting data externally to Edelman's (2007) image of the brain as a complex jungle ecosystem. Sylwester (1995) states: "teachers become facilitators, who help to shape a stimulating social environment that helps students to work alone and together to solve the problems they confront". This underpins the key intent of the IB learner profile—to encourage schools to review the philosophy, structures and systems to enable lifelong learners to develop. This does mean questioning the range of strategies for learning, the central role of the teacher as facilitator and the extent to which we question the learning processes in a 21st-century context.

As Sylwester (1995) points out:

> Current brain theory and research now provide only the broad, tantalizing outlines of what the school of the future might be … Educators who are willing to study the new cognitive science developments … will have to work out the specifics in the years ahead. If our profession doesn't do it, nothing will happen. Things will remain as they are.

An analysis of our developing understanding of the science of the brain appears to demonstrate several key brain-based principles.

- **Learning is enhanced by challenge and inhibited by threat**—a rich range of activities in a stimulating environment (having established a state of relaxed alertness) will enable the mind to engage more readily in problem-solving and pattern understanding. Anxiety, threat and inducing an atmosphere of stress will result in the "fight, flight or freeze" response of the reptilian brain, leading to little, if any, constructive learning.
- **Cognition and emotion are difficult to separate**—our memory is enhanced through emotional connection and inquiry may be developed through positive risk-taking and intriguing open-questioning.
- **Learning involves both focused attention and peripheral perception**—our jungle-system brains are continuously processing information received through our senses, thus a rich visual environment can support focused and targeted learning programmes.
- **Each brain is unique**—this reflects the movements from a mass transmission model of learning to a customized individual inquiry approach that embeds lifelong learning skills.

Certainly a key principle for our teachers is that a raised self-awareness of the individual pathways to learning can be enhanced through an increased understanding of brain-based approaches.

To what extent does your current brain knowledge influence your learning?

What kind of brain-based learner are you?

Key questions

How might we develop brain-based approaches in the classroom?

How does the range of strategies we adopt meet the unique nature of each learner?

How might we encourage leaders to further develop expertise in this important area?

The way forward

This has just been a start, and one that we hope might encourage further reading in this important aspect of our different approaches to learning. This might involve the exploration of the impact of diet and exercise on the brain or the importance of specialist programmes such as Brain Gym® or HeartMath to encourage a positive impact on our physiology and, consequently, on our brain processes. You may also wish to focus on areas such as the influence of music on the brain's processes.

As stated at the outset of this chapter, we are in the relative foothills of the region of comprehending the brain and the continuing development of imaging techniques will mean that our understanding and ability to use new knowledge will extend rapidly. As educators, we need to be aware of these developments and be alert enough to adapt new knowledge to enhance the learning process.

Richard Restak (2003) points out in his book *The New Brain*:

> *Our brain's organisation will undergo greater changes during the next several decades than at any time in our history ... Most important, the changes in our brains brought about by technology will continue to provide us with the challenge of retaining our freedom and sense of identity while simultaneously utilising soon to be available techniques to vastly expand our mental horizons.*

The challenges now for educators at all levels are to stay informed, explore current practices in the light of developing understanding and, as in an effective lesson, continue to examine the connections between the brain and our environment, feelings and thought—all of which forms a meaningful learning experience.

CHAPTER 3

The individuality of the learner

I hear and I forget;
I see and I remember;
I do and I understand.

Ancient Chinese proverb

In the 21st century the prime purpose of school should be to develop independent, self-managing learners with the basic knowledge and skills which adequately prepare them for the challenges they will face in their futures ... They should be knowledgeable about their own individual talents and how to use them effectively.

(Hood 2006)

In this new century we increasingly have the opportunity to customize or personalize our leisure pursuits, select and group our own music, access television programmes and films on demand and instantly communicate with friends in distant parts of the world. In spite of these technological and knowledge shifts, many schools maintain the structures of learning from over 100 years ago—with similar age grouping, linear progression and mass instruction, based on the beliefs that students of a similar age should be able to learn in the same way and at the same pace.

With the growing personalization of many aspects of our changing world, together with significant recent developments in understanding the brain's relationship to the learning processes, we continue to move towards an increased understanding of the uniqueness of each learner. Therefore, as we continue to explore the world of learning we should perhaps be open to examining the notions of diversity and individual learning styles and the implications for teachers, learning environments and assessment methodologies.

Our education systems of recent centuries have emphasized linguistic and mathematical skills, suitable to the world of that time. Research in more recent years focuses on developing students' self-awareness to enable them to grow into flexible, lifelong learners. The learners of the 21st century require an effective range of communication, problem-solving and team skills to be self-motivated and engaged in the learning process throughout their lives.

This chapter aims to outline the debate surrounding the developing understanding of learning styles, multiple intelligences and how self-awareness impacts upon curriculum and the role of the teacher.

Examples of the blurring of subject knowledge into a more direct "learning to learn" approach are increasingly prevalent, with a greater focus on personalizing learning motivation.

CASE STUDY

GABRIEL SOLARI/ST XAVIER'S COLLEGE/BUENOS AIRES/MIDDLE YEARS PROGRAMME (YEAR 3)

Interdisciplinary activities: mathematics, literature and history

Investigation on cryptography

The objective of this task is to provide the students with the opportunity to study how one concept (in this case cryptography) can be related to different fields of human knowledge such as literature, mathematics and history.

The student should read *The Gold Bug*, a short story by Edgar Allan Poe, in which the main character (Mr Legrand) finds an encyphered message that leads to a treasure that pirates have buried on an island.

The message contains strange symbols, and Mr Legrand supposes that every symbol corresponds to a letter from the English alphabet.

He goes on to calculate the relative frequency of every symbol (that is, working out the percentage of the times it appears in the whole text) and compares them with one of the letters in different English texts.

He assumes that it is most likely that the symbol with the highest frequency corresponds to the letter with the highest frequency.

This method soon encounters some problems, so he then studies what three-symbol "words" are most common in the text and compares them to the words "the" and "and". By combining both methods he is finally able to break the code.

So far, the student is able to see the cryptography in a fictional context, through the world of literature.

After having this first contact, the students are invited to try it out themselves, by checking with a short text that the basics of Mr Legrand's method show some consistency.

Now we turn to the real world.

The student must carry out research of his or her own into two historical events in which cryptography played an essential role: the beheading of Mary, Queen of Scots, and the breaking of the German Enigma code.

If they are interested in the topic, we suggest that they continue the research with other ideas, such as the short story *The Dancing Men* by Arthur Conan Doyle, the deciphering of the Rosetta stone by Champollion (the key to understanding Egyptian hieroglyphics) or the cipher disc of Julius Caesar.

Learning styles—experiential models

Much of the development in the use of learning styles stems from the work of David Kolb, who published his Learning Styles model in 1984 in his book *Experiential Learning*. His learning theory refers to four distinct learning styles, based on a four-stage learning cycle (Figure 3.1). The cycle begins with immediate or concrete "experiences that provide a basis for observations and reflections", which are assimilated and distilled into "abstract concepts" that lead to new implications for action that can be "actively tested". This in turn creates new experiences. Thus, Kolb views the learning process as being a flow of experiencing, reflecting, thinking and acting.

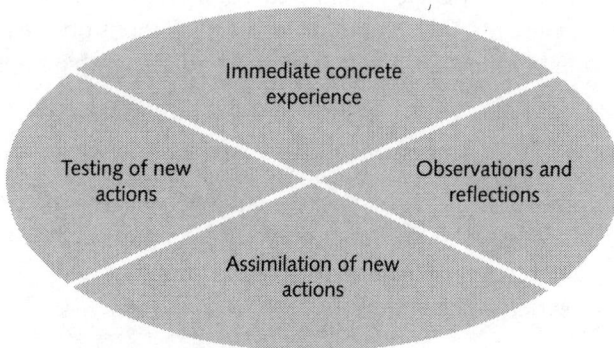

Figure 3.1: Kolb's four-stage learning cycle

Kolb goes on to develop this experiential learning cycle to explain the natural learning preferences of different people via a behavioural and personality model, using the following learning styles definitions.

▶ **Diverging learners** prefer to focus on feeling the experience and then reflect upon it. They tend to be people who are imaginative and emotional, preferring to work in groups.

▶ **Assimilating learners** prefer a logical approach, with clear explanation. They perform well at taking in and ordering significant amounts of information. They prefer reading and formal lectures and are not particularly fond of working in groups.

▶ **Converging learners** tend to be more practical and are essentially doers and problem-solvers. They are particularly interested in technical tasks.

▶ **Accommodating learners** rely more on intuition, often acting on gut instinct rather than logical analysis. Such learners prefer to work in teams and to be involved actively to achieve objectives.

By increasing awareness of the individuality of our learners' profiles and approaches we can increase our range of strategies to underpin relationships in the classroom.

CASE STUDY

Samah Hidaya/Ahliyyah School for Girls/Amman, Jordan

Arabic strategies (IB Diploma Programme)

Building a student's personal portfolio is an essential strategy that I depend on while teaching Arabic on the Diploma Programme. The portfolio can be a useful and creative learning tool that helps students organize and review their work. Students are required to insert into the portfolio their observations, comments, interpretations and explanations on the relevant documents, whether they are drama, poetry, short stories, biographies or literature.

The students keep their homework and assessed work in their portfolios.

The portfolio grows daily. Accordingly, the students become more aware of the learning process they go through and they mature as they follow up their learning and recognize the importance of using their self-assessment to promote their own learning strategies.

The portfolio enables them to build on their strengths and to overcome their weaknesses. In time they develop into confident, lifelong learners.

Arabic strategies (middle school)

AHMAD ZALAT/ARABIC TEACHER/AHLIYYAH SCHOOL FOR GIRLS/AMMAN, JORDAN

To expose students to a wide scope of literature and to help them analyse and criticize literary work and to enhance their writing and verbal expression the following strategy is used.

One assigned novel is read by all students and it is discussed during Arabic classes in the first term. During the second term the class is divided into five or six groups and each group is assigned a novel that is presented to the class in written form. The group members then discuss it with their classmates, who have been instructed to read it previously. Accordingly, each student would read five or six novels per academic year.

Choosing a poem and presenting it to the class with a brief introduction about the poet is also a strategy that I often use in my classes.

Each student chooses a poem, recites it in front of an audience, justifies his or her choice and introduces the main theme of the poem. This will expose the students to a large number of poems and poets and enable them to communicate with an audience. This activity encourages the students to form their opinions and to defend their choices. It enhances their linguistic and literary skills in addition to promoting their reciting skills and their ability to reciprocate with an audience.

Kolb's (1984) ideas led to various models, most notably Honey and Mumford's view of four learning types:

► **Activists** seek instant experience and are generally outgoing.
► **Pragmatists** try out ideas and enjoy problem-solving.
► **Reflectors** gather data, stand back and think before acting.
► **Theorists** draw conclusions and think things through in logical steps.

One can see that both Kolb's (1984) and Honey and Mumford's (1986) theories reflect aspects of left/right brain hemisphere predominances. Similarly, Felder and Silverman's (2005) Index of Learning Styles focuses on four dimensions, with a continuum between right and left, as shown in Figure 3.2.

A series of self-review questions enable you to assess a place on the continuum, with a view to developing a balanced approach and maximizing the ability to absorb and effectively use information. A key aspect of

Sensory Look for facts	⟵⟶	**Intuitive** Look for meaning
Visual Pictures, visual representations, mind maps	⟵⟶	**Verbal** Hear or read with explanation from words
Active Work in groups Physically manipulate objects	⟵⟶	**Reflective** Think things through and work out problems alone
Sequential Information taken in by orderly process Create big picture from details	⟵⟶	**Global** Prefer a holistic approach—seeing the big picture and then providing details

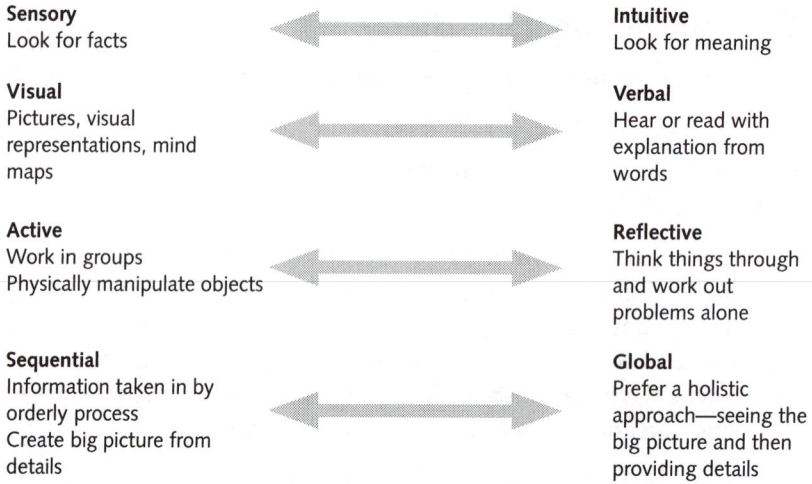

Figure 3.2: Felder and Silverman's (2005) Index of Learning Styles dimensions

the behaviourist approach to learning styles is that preferences vary for each of us in different situations but that through understanding and self-awareness you can extend your style and increase your learning skills.

Reflection

Based on the theories of Kolb, and Honey and Mumford, what learning style do you most identify with?

Do you think you tend to make use of your preferred learning style when delivering to your students?

How might you meet the needs of both sequential and global learners in a particular lesson?

How might you vary strategies and student groupings to meet the needs of activists, pragmatists, reflectors and theorists?

To what extent are your colleagues aware of their own learning preferences?

Visual, auditory, kinaesthetic

Much of the original work on visual, auditory, kinaesthetic (VAK) dates back to psychologists and teachers such as Fernald, Keller, Orton, Stillman and Montessori, beginning in the 1920s, and VAK has now become very much a part of the accelerated learning movement. The principles of VAK provide a different perspective on the sensory modalities view of how the learner takes in and understands information. As with the behavioural-ist approach, this is not an attempt to label the learner as a type. VAK helps raise student and teacher awareness of the need to ensure a range of sensory stimulating and engaging strategies that will match student preferences. As Barbara Prashnig (1998) notes:

> *As long as teaching methods are not individualised and teachers continue to use identical strategies for everyone, knowing they are only effective for some, they will not reach those who need it most and will keep losing them.*

If we explore VAK we can see that there are opportunities for teachers to vary a range of teaching strategies, including the effective use of the learning environment, in order to stimulate the senses across a range of learning preferences. There is also a range of questionnaires, both paper based and online, that quickly enable learners of all ages to identify potential preferences, such as those below.

Learning Style	Preference	
Visual	Seeing, reading, pictures—stimulus through colour, shape, display	
Auditory	Listening, speaking, debate, lectures	
Kinaesthetic	Touching and doing, moving, acting	

Some schools of thought suggest that current educational systems should focus on a movement through kinaesthetics in the early years with an emphasis on play or doing, through the visual of the middle years with its focus on reading and visual presentation, on to the later years of degree study and its reliance upon the auditory experience of the lecture theatre and seminar room. This is the reality of learning at all ages and there is a need for acceptance and awareness of preferences and to ensure that teachers are conscious of the need to vary teaching and learning strategies to satisfy all styles.

CASE STUDY

Gabriel Solari/St Xavier's College/Buenos Aires, Argentina

Some experiences dealing with kinaesthetic intelligence in mathematics

I came up with the following activities to try to involve the students' own bodies in the process of understanding mathematical ideas.

Chess knights and linear function in the playground

In case some students did not know how the movement of a chess knight works, I asked some of the other students to explain the eight possible "L-shape" movements.

Then we went to the school's playground, where we fixed two long, perpendicular rolls of paper representing the X- and Y-axes with a point marked every 90 cm or so. By doing this we transformed the playground into the Cartesian plane.

I asked one of the students to stand on the point where the axes intersect (the centre of the Cartesian plane), and then he had to choose one of the knight's movements and move accordingly. Then another student was invited to stand next to the first, and walk from that point following the same knight movement.

I repeated the procedure with five students, who were in the same line when the activity finished. The students represented points of the Cartesian plane that belong to the same line.

So I asked them different questions, such as
- ▶ What shape is formed by the students?
- ▶ If the first student had chosen another knight movement, what changes would we have had?

Then I asked another student to start the process again, choosing another knight movement, and we compared the different angles formed by the line made by the students.

Basically, the eight movements can be reduced to four in this context, with two of the students developing lines forming an acute angle with the X-axis and the other two an obtuse angle.

The activity helped students to understand the concept of "gradient of a linear function" and also to see the differences between a positive and a negative gradient.

The activity continued with me asking another student to stand on another point of the Y-axis and repeat the procedure again. Now the concept of "Y-intercept of a linear function" appeared. The line is displaced in parallel way with the original line; the lines still form the same angle with the X-axis (they have the same gradient) but they cut the Y-axis at different points (they have a different Y-intercept).

Drawing parabolas and lines on the playground

The idea was basically the same but now the students represented lines with their bodies.

The class was divided into groups of five.

I gave them the formula for a quadratic equation. They were asked to represent five points of the parabola that matched the formula.

When they finished I asked them to move one step to the right (or to the left, or upwards, or downwards) and then asked them, "what is the equation of the new parabola?".

I then gave them a new equation and asked them to move in order to form the parabola corresponding to the equation.

The idea of this activity is to make students "feel" what happens to the points on a parabola if the equation changes.

Lines and parabolas meet each other

The class was divided into two groups.

One of the groups was given the equation for a line and the other group the equation for a parabola.

I asked them to represent the functions for some specific values of X.

Previously, I had chosen two curves that intersect at one point, so two students should stay in the same place.

Then I asked these two students for the coordinates that correspond to their position, these being the solution of the simultaneous equations involving the two curves.

I'd like to add just two comments.

Some weeks after doing this activity, one of the students had a query about an exercise relating to the gradient of a line and one of his classmates explained the solution to him and added "I understood this when we had the chess activity in the playground".

I felt happy listening to him because, evidently, the activity had been meaningful for his understanding of the linear function.

I tried these experiences with different groups of experienced maths teachers, and most of them found some difficulty in following the "drawing of the parabola". Even when they understand perfectly well the concepts involved, they had problems in "connecting their bodies with their minds" in the activity.

Examples of visual learning would particularly involve the use of diagrams, demonstrations, displays, handouts, films, slide displays, memory maps, flow charts and story boards. For auditory learning the focus would be on listening skills, audio tapes, paired discussion, debate, raps, rhymes and chants. The kinaesthetic learner will benefit through physical experience—visits, field trips, gestures, interactive software and role play. It is interesting to note that, frequently, children with particular learning needs tend to be kinaesthetic learners yet generally experience a teaching model that focuses on visual or auditory approaches.

The value of matching teaching to learning preferences may be seen as more important when dealing with complex learning problems. Some teachers believe in encouraging students to be aware of styles other than their particular preference. In developing lifelong learning skills, it appears to be important to raise self-awareness in order to encourage motivation and esteem in the learner.

Following on the work of Dunn and Dunn (1978), Barbara Prashnig (1998), in her work *The Power of Diversity*, notes:

> If people are allowed to learn and work through their own styles and find suitable environments for their activities, there is no limit to what human beings can achieve, and they can actually do it with much less stress and much more joy.

She bases her research and recommendation on the Dunns' definition of a learning style as "the way in which human beings begin to concentrate on, absorb, process and retain new and difficult information". Prashnig focuses on six key areas of the learning styles profile. These are shown in Figure 3.3.

She goes on to explain that through learning, teaching and working style analysis tools one can see that brain dominance, sensory modalities,

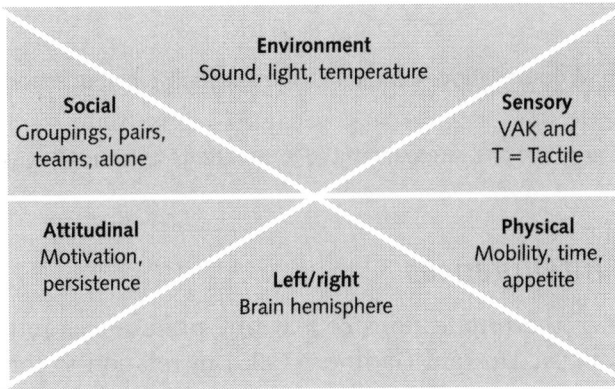

Figure 3.3: Prashnig's six key areas of learning

physical needs and environmental preferences are essentially biological givens and are unlikely to change significantly. Where these are matched to appropriate teaching styles they will enable fast learning success. Social and attitudinal groupings are, she notes, essentially conditioning, are not as stable and tend to reflect changes in the world around you. Where used wisely, they can become a significant strength and underpin motivation to learn effectively.

Key questions

Why might VAK awareness be important for teachers?

How could such an awareness improve student–teacher relationships?

In what ways might VAK understanding aid study skills?

Prashnig argues that a raised awareness of learning styles leads to improved relationships and a stronger focus on high-quality work. She notes Glasser's message identifying the six conditions for quality schoolwork:

▶ There is a warm, supportive learning environment.

▶ The work is relevant and purposeful.

▶ Students are always encouraged to do the best they can.

▶ Students are asked to evaluate and improve their own work.

▶ Quality work feels good.

▶ Quality work is never destructive.

Multiple intelligences

Any review of the implications of learning preferences must take note of the work of Dr Howard Gardner (1993) in relation to the concept of multiple intelligences (MIs) and their potential impact on the learning process.

Howard Gardner and his Harvard team have, since the early 1980s, postulated the theory of different forms of intelligence, with primarily eight different forms. These are described below.

Verbal/linguistic (word smart)

Shown through writing, imagery and symbolic thinking—a skill that can be improved by increased opportunities to speak, tell stories, play word memory games, debate and discuss.

Logical/mathematical (number smart)

Indicates the ability to recognize patterns and see connections—this can be enhanced in students through data analysis, stepped approaches to problem-solving, and using spreadsheets and deduction puzzles.

As noted previously, verbal/linguistic and logical/mathematical intelligences form the basis of many educational systems and most forms of standardized testing regimes.

Visual/spatial (picture smart)

The visual arts, map-making, architecture, looking at objects from different perspectives and angles—this can be developed by using learning posters/memory maps, diagrams, and colour for highlighting.

Bodily/kinaesthetic (body smart)

Using the body to express feeling and emotion, through dance, sporting ability and learning through doing—developed by practical activities, such as act-out learning, making models and using brain breaks ("calming down" exercises after physical activity to refocus concentration and enable reflection, thus allowing information to be absorbed).

Musical/rhythmic (music smart)

Recognizing and using rhythm and tonal patterns, aiding memory and influencing feeling through music. Lessons may use rapping or chants, and music can be used to calm, energize or mark points of learning. Try listening to Korsakov's "Flight of the Bumblebee" before tidying away after a practical lesson.

Interpersonal (people smart)

Able to work cooperatively as part of a team, good communicator, shows empathy—skills usually developed in counsellors, teachers and therapists. We can develop this intelligence through working in groups/teams, with pair-and-share activities, partner discussion and students teaching each other.

Intrapersonal (self smart)

Understanding oneself, feelings, the ability to step back and reflect, the art of metacognition. An increasingly important skill in seeing the wholeness of parts—looking for a sense of unity—an intelligence prominent in philosophy. A skill to be developed through activities such as Philosophy for Children—offering open questions, time for reflection, the opportunity to work independently and select the way forward from a series of choices.

Naturalistic (nature smart)

The ability to appreciate the world of nature—a sense of wonder and awe at phenomena of the natural world. An intelligence often seen in farmers, gardeners, cooks and veterinarians.

As with VAK, the importance of the multiple intelligences lies in the development of self-awareness and the challenge to extend the range of learning opportunities to meet the varying needs of our students (Figure 3.4).

As David Lazear (2001) points out:

> One of the exciting things about teaching with multiple intelligences is that there is not just one right way to do it. There are many right ways! In fact, the only limits in planning lessons that incorporate multiple intelligences are your own creativity and willingness to experiment with the teaching/learning process in your classroom.

Visual | Auditory | Kinaesthetic

Multiple Intelligences

Most learning takes place when we see, say and do something

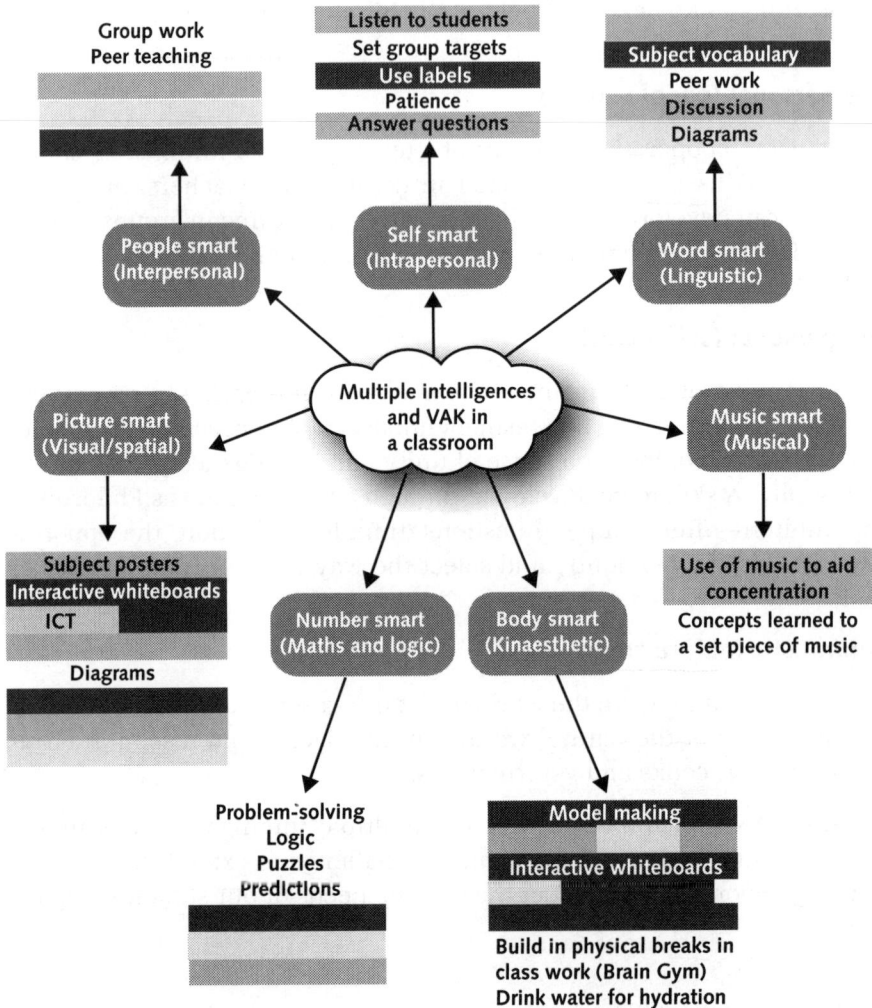

Group work
Peer teaching

Listen to students
Set group targets
Use labels
Patience
Answer questions

Subject vocabulary
Peer work
Discussion
Diagrams

People smart
(Interpersonal)

Self smart
(Intrapersonal)

Word smart
(Linguistic)

Picture smart
(Visual/spatial)

Multiple intelligences
and VAK in
a classroom

Music smart
(Musical)

Subject posters
Interactive whiteboards
ICT

Diagrams

Number smart
(Maths and logic)

Body smart
(Kinaesthetic)

Use of music to aid
concentration

Concepts learned to
a set piece of music

Problem-solving
Logic
Puzzles
Predictions

Model making

Interactive whiteboards

Build in physical breaks in
class work (Brain Gym)
Drink water for hydration

Figure 3.4: MI and VAK in a classroom

A key part of the process must be the raising of awareness across the school community, involving pupils and parents in exploring their own learning preferences and emphasizing that each of us possesses a unique fingerprint of learning.

CASE STUDY

DANIEL PENN/BROUGHTON HALL HIGH SCHOOL/LIVERPOOL, UK

Learning preferences and multiple intelligences

Broughton Hall High School in Liverpool is an all-girls' Catholic High School for 11- to 18-year-olds in the suburbs of Liverpool. The school has 1,275 students, covering all levels of ability.

Broughton Hall has been involved in a range of national and international projects focusing on challenging assumptions about the way people learn, seeking to provide learning opportunities which are relevant, engaging and challenging.

For the past six years the school has explored the impact of learning preferences and multiple intelligences—known to students as "learning smarts". Before students enter the school they are questioned and examined to seek an indication of VAK and MI preferences. Girls attend a learning conference, where they experience the range of VAK and MI approaches and make a colour icon-coded card, which indicates their learning and MI preferences. The focus is not on labelling students but rather on raising student, teacher and parent awareness of the different ways we learn. Girls keep their cards with them and information on VAK and MI preferences is passed to all teaching staff.

Through this awareness all students know they have the capacity to learn and tackle challenges put to them, while teachers are aware of the range of preferences and are able to adapt strategies to match them. Some teachers adopt home and away groups of students by either joining or mixing students of similar MIs. Students are also encouraged to make use of alternative preferences to extend their learning styles.

Students can be retested to note changes and developments in styles and MIs. A wide range of strategies are available on line for teachers to adapt, and teachers in many subject areas have rewritten work to ensure that preferences are reflected in a wide range of strategies. Students have undertaken research into the use and impact of "smart cards" on their own learning and have made recommendations to the teachers to ensure that they are used to the maximum effect.

The key impacts have been on raising awareness of the uniqueness of each learner and the need to ensure that we adopt a wide range of strategies and aim to match them to student preferences.

In the world of education, where the focus in the past has largely been on well-developed linguistic and logical approaches led by teachers who have succeeded via this route, it is important to approach with an open mind the multiple intelligences and the opportunities they provide for a multi-sensory, challenging and engaging range of learning strategies. This is perhaps more particularly apt now in our changing world, where interpersonal, naturalistic and problem-solving skills are gaining in importance as our young people are increasingly required to be flexible and able to sustain lifelong learning motivation.

In examining approaches to individual learning preferences it is important to keep certain key principles in mind:

- ▶ Learning preferences may vary from one learning topic to another.
- ▶ Pupil and teacher self-awareness is critical—avoid accepting given assumptions.
- ▶ Our rapidly developing world of technology is impacting upon learning styles.
- ▶ Deeper, more effective learning is achieved when we appreciate each other's differences.

An awareness of the individuality of the learning process can help in the development of the teacher—student relationship, which is fundamental to effective long-term learning. Also, as we strive to develop our students as lifelong learners, an increased self-awareness of individual learning strengths can only help to enhance our continuing motivation to grow as problem-solvers with the confidence, self-worth and initiative to face the challenges of the 21st century.

CHAPTER 4
Thinking about learning, learning about thinking

Give a person a fish and you feed him for a day, teach a person to fish and you feed him for a lifetime.

Chinese proverb

In this chapter we explore the principles and applications of thinking skills and how they form a key element of the lifelong learning skills required by our young people.

In order to build on ideas outlined in Chapter 2, in which we undertook a review of the influence of the brain on our learning processes, it is important to explore the areas of the brain in action through thinking skills. We begin with an approach to defining thinking skills and their relevance and moving through practical examples of how the various forms of thinking development can profoundly affect lifelong learning skills.

As early as 1916, Dewey was pointing to a key purpose for our schools:

... all which the school can or need do for students, so far as their minds are concerned, is to develop the ability to think.

Perhaps the earliest references to the development of a range of thinking skills are those of the ancient Greeks. Socrates was a provider of problem-solving opportunities for his students, seeking to develop their thinking skills through "dialogue" between the expert and the students. He sought to draw out from within through the mediation of questioning and prompting, thus enabling students to discuss and expand ideas among themselves. The methodology of posing a problem and encouraging mediated dialogue to draw out solutions may be seen as a fundamental part of the thinking skills process—a process vital to the development of lifelong learning skills.

Plato, a student of Socrates, extended this approach through the questioning of held beliefs tested by logic and reasoning. This focus on logic linked to philosophy, mathematics and physics is a central aspect of critical thinking approaches. Aristotle, a student of Plato, played a key role in establishing many of the fundamental principles of logic.

The beginnings of the links between our reasoning brain and thinking processes go back to the writings of Descartes in the 17th century and his famous phrase, "I think therefore I am". Much of our developing understanding of cognitive science has been built on this foundation, leading on to the work of Piaget and Vygotsky. Both born in 1896, these two psychologists developed much of the 20th-century view on thinking in learning, though from different standpoints. Piaget emphasized learners' cognitive development as they interact with the world around them, while Vygotsky focused on societal influence, emphasizing the importance of language in shaping learners' thinking. The work of Dr Reuven Feuerstein has also had a profound effect on the development of thinking skills. Working with traumatized Jewish adolescents, he focused on effective mediation using "Instruments of Enrichment" to develop specific skills of categorization and analysis and to encourage metacognition—thinking about thinking.

The IB learner profile introduction points to the need for "IB programmes to promote ... independent critical and creative thought". The learner profile also points to the importance of reflection by the teacher, student and organization—a critical skill often lacking in a world of exponential change.

In order to fulfil the IB mission of developing "internationally minded people", the focus on extending reflective and thinking skills may be seen as of critical importance. The IB learner profile promotes the development of our students as "inquirers" and an increased awareness of the principles and techniques of thinking skills can enhance that learning process. An embedding of critical and creative thinking skills can encourage an independence and enjoyment of learning motivated by inquiry; an independence that can be sustained throughout our learning lives.

CASE STUDY

Faten Saloum/grade 3 teacher/Ahliyyah School for Girls/Amman, Jordan

Strategies related to IB learner profile (elementary school)

I have been a Grade 3 home-room teacher for the past 11 years.

I can say that focusing on the IB profile made me more aware of the fact that the young people I am teaching can be helped to become more aware of their potential as knowledgeable thinkers and lifelong, creative learners.

I create investigative activities in my science, maths, social studies and language lessons. These activities facilitate the discovery process that my students go through; these activities also help them to think of the different possible variables that they can apply in order to construct their knowledge base. I allow ample time to help them reflect on their constructed knowledge. I focus, too, on hands-on activities that help them build a sound language register and to continuously enlarge this register in all the areas of knowledge that I teach. (As an example, my students are able to visualize the meaning of authority, logic and variable ... and are able to express and apply their understanding of these terms in various forms.)

Another key area for development concerns our students as "thinkers" — able to make reasoned, ethical decisions. This requires an understanding of the effective application of a range of thinking skills approaches to challenge our students, in order to develop the vital 21st-century skills of initiative, teamwork, perseverance and problem-solving.

A further aspect of the profile most closely associated with thinking skills is that of the reflective learner. This, an aspect often missing from many educational processes, is another important element of thinking skills as we provide opportunities for metacognition, thinking about our learning, to enable our students to challenge assumptions and to better understand their own learning and thinking processes.

An effective approach to developing critical and creative thinking skills can therefore be seen to underpin the aims, principles and processes of the IB learner profile and plays a central role in the development of lifelong learning skills.

The aim of education should be to teach us how to think rather than what to think ... to improve our minds, so as to enable us to think for ourselves rather than to load the memory with the thoughts of other men.

(Dewey 1916)

CASE STUDY

Nasri Khader Tarazi/Ahliyyah School for Girls/Amman, Jordan

Mathematics (Grades 1–12)

I was inspired by the usefulness of investigations in helping students reflect and make the required connections in an active and meaningful manner as opposed to listening to a lecture or even sitting in a class where the teacher interacts with students while explaining the topic at hand. I have, therefore, designed some introductory worksheets that help the students understand the topic to be presented before the teaching begins proper. Those worksheets are not investigations in the sense that they:

▶ do not meet the assessment criteria of the IB
▶ can be very short
▶ are not usually assessed.

However, the worksheets contain an investigative element in the sense that they present a problem or a question that the student cannot yet answer based on a previous study. The theme is developed slowly and thus a student "investigates" an issue.

The students take the worksheets and go through the leading questions at home to discover a principle, rule or concept. In the following lesson, I go through the questions with them. We discuss their answers and how they thought about the questions and highlight the major ideas.

Generally, I find that a new topic is made a lot easier for both teachers and students if it is treated in this way. Better understanding is reached, less time is needed and more fruitful discussion takes place.

I would like to believe that this relates to the IB learner profile in that it contributes in helping the students strive to be inquirers, knowledgeable, thinkers, communicators, reflective and even risk takers. Furthermore, this helps train them on the investigations required for the internal assessment.

Today, more than ever, our students need to develop the skills of classifying, prioritizing and synthesizing information—understanding what is relevant, what to discard and how to present that information to a range of possible audiences.

As Adey and Shayer (1994) point out:

> It is not what students learn, but how they learn it, that matters.
> How they learn depends on their cognitive processing capability
> and intervention in the process by which this capability develops is
> the route to fundamental improved life chances in the population
> of learners.

The focus in the 21st century has shifted from simply knowing and repeating information (i.e. knowledge passed by transmission processes) to understanding how to learn and how to find out relevant information and develop skills of using that information appropriately. Our young people face a life of continued learning during which they will be required to exhibit the skills of creative thinking, developing ideas, engaging in reasoned argument and solving problems—individually and as part of a team—and continuing to develop as thinkers, workers, citizens and people through the skill of reflection.

As Hoffer (1942) states:

> *In times of change the learners will inherit the world—while the knowers will find themselves beautifully equipped to deal with a world that no longer exists.*

CASE STUDY

Khalida Qattash and Badiah Madbak/Ahliyyah School for Girls/Amman, Jordan

Theory of knowledge

Theory of knowledge (TOK) is a course that takes time to soak in on the part of students; therefore, methods used in teaching this course must essentially be based on interactive strategies, so that students are gradually brought to feel its relevance to their lives. Moreover, since TOK requires a knowledge base that needs to be acquired through reading and exposure to a variety of materials, theories, philosophical approaches and so on, methods employed should be based on drawing on students' own experiences and interests, and incorporating them within the class activities. Accordingly, one method used to do so is to prepare an open-ended lesson plan. The lesson plan is based on introducing a basic concept in addition to exposing students to relevant materials to be read partially in class. However, the core examples that are to be drawn, in an attempt to embody this concept, are ones derived from students' own experiences and interests. For example, students are asked to relate the difference between *certainty* and *belief* to examples of their own choice. If their own choice is to base their comparison on a theme such as *love*, the lesson will take this path and utilize their chosen theme to its utmost. This requires a lot of effort on the part of the teacher, who must be fully aware of his or her students at an individual level, in addition to being well read and possessing the ability to critically and openly respond to students' ideas and incorporate them within the theme central to the lesson. Challenging, yet interesting enough, students gradually are drawn into appreciating and utilizing such a course in their own thinking and lives.

Key questions

How might we currently define thinking skills?

To what extent are such skills integrated into current learning delivery?

Should thinking skills be delivered as a topic in its own right or as an embedded part of the learning process?

How might thinking for learning support other skills such as literacy, collaboration, questioning and cognitive processing?

How might thinking skills develop student understanding?

Defining thinking

In 1910 Dewey defined thinking as:

> *That operation in which present facts suggest other facts (or truths) in such a way as to induce belief in the latter upon the ground or warrant of the former.*

He believed that effective thinking was "active, persistent and careful consideration", built upon the foundation of "correct habits of reflection". He sees "bad thinking" as unquestioning acceptance of suggestion without analysing evidence, whereas

> *Good thinkers maintain the state of doubt and carry on systematic and protracted inquiry ... there are the essentials of thinking.*

The significance of developing challenging thinking and questioning must be seen in the context of the belief that a child's intelligence is not fixed, but that through the development of effective learning habits cognitive ability can be extended.

Feuerstein argues that "the human organism is open to modifiability at all ages and stages of development". The focus of Feuerstein's Instrumental Enrichment (FIE) is the identification and mediation of specific thinking approaches in order to improve cognitive ability. These phases of thinking may be seen as the identification of a problem, the gathering of evidence and the arrival at a conclusion.

These phases of critical thinking may be seen to reflect the learning skills for life required more than ever in the rapidly changing complex world. These would appear to include effective skills of literacy and numeracy, as well as the ability to work with others and to deal with constant change. They would also include the ability to research and gather information and to adopt a positive and flexible approach to a range of different problems, to develop effective communication skills, to listen and respond critically but positively to and with others in a variety of disciplines and situations and to be able to make decisions and follow through outcomes in an appropriate manner.

Key questions

When and how in your classroom/school are opportunities created to develop the skills outlined above?

Are those skills infused into learning opportunities or made explicit as a set of identifiable strategies?

Are those skills developed in theory or in practical, relevant and engaging activities?

How do you measure the impact of the development of such learning skills?

How might your students carry those skills into their lives outside school?

The development of problem-solving or critical thinking skills may be seen to be linked to what psychologists refer to as "propositioned" thought, that is where we hear language and order and structure words to form reasoned argument. We are also subject to "imaginal" thought, where visual images enter our minds and are often used for visualization or creative tasks. We are thinking all the time in different ways, but it is how we understand the key principles of "thinking for learning" that helps us and our students to focus that process in order to explore, create and understand the world we inhabit.

We may therefore define a range of thinking skills, such as those outlined in Figure 4.1.

From this figure one could identify many skills—such as ordering, weighing pros and cons and prioritizing—that are extremely important in our knowledge society where we have access to so much information at the click of a mouse.

The principles and characteristics of thinking for learning

An appreciation of the effectiveness of the development of thinking skills for learning can be seen to be founded on several key principles and characteristics.

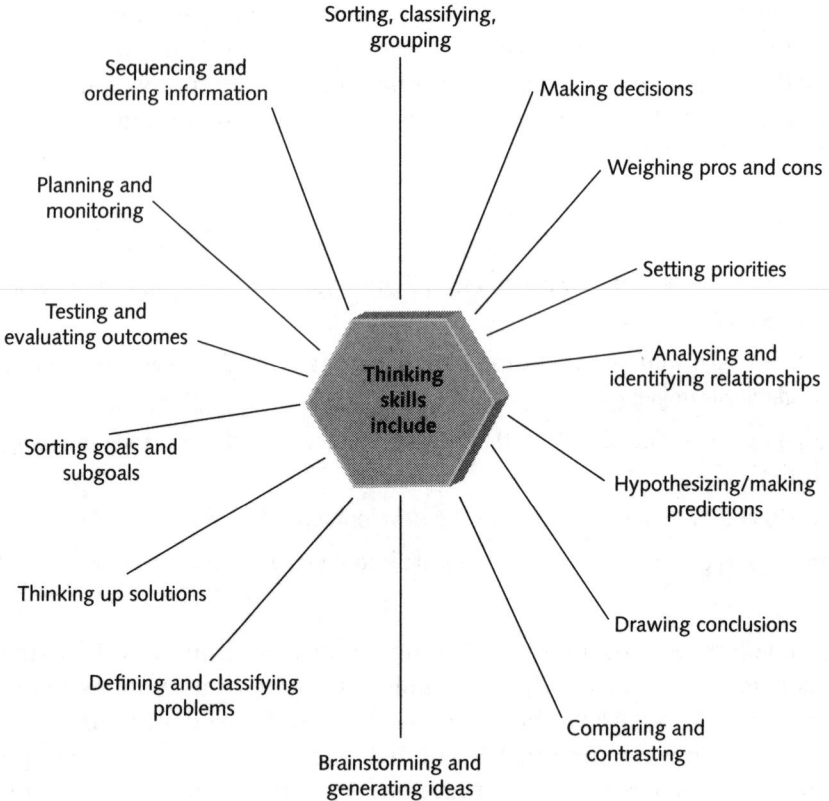

Figure 4.1: Thinking skills

▶ Children's intelligence is not fixed. It can be modified and
  strengthened by the development of learning strategies, which
  can be carried forward into challenges of our rapidly changing
  21st century.

▶ Mediation is an essential part of teaching, and thinking for
  learning extends that mediation role as a guide and prompter
  rather than transmitter of given knowledge.

▶ Challenge, interest and relevance are key to the development
  of thinking for learning. We must take our students beyond the
  immediate and develop them through access to a range of wider
  experiences.

These principles and characteristics may then be identified in a range
of processes and strategies that can be explicitly employed or embedded
as part of the learning curriculum. By identifying these characteristics,
however, we make our teachers and students more aware of the need to
build on the range of learning tools.

▶ Students and teachers are encouraged to think and talk about learning. Learning and the strategies to improve lie at the heart of the relationship between student and teacher.

▶ Thinking for learning encourages the development of explicit learning strategies. Opportunities are created for students and teachers to discuss the effectiveness of a range of strategies that can be employed in different learning situations.

▶ Thinking for learning encourages the principle of participation. Contributions are valid to the process of understanding and explanation in both critical and creative thinking.

▶ Through these key principles of involvement, reflection, mediation and articulation, the opportunity to bridge those skills to all areas of learning is enhanced, providing explicit lifelong learning skills to face the challenges of the world today.

Processes of thinking for learning

These principles and characteristics can be put into practice through a series of appropriate processes, which can be outlined as follows:

▶ Learning is a social activity. Enhanced understanding comes through dialogue—listening to and understanding others. As Lipman (2003) states, "learning behaviour for thinking is talking".

▶ There is a need to be reflective, through metacognition—thinking about our thinking to embed those skills and use in a range of contexts.

▶ The importance of seeing connections, inferences, meanings, patterns and relationships beyond the immediate. Daniel H Pink may refer to this as the art of symphony—the drawing together of elements to create a greater sense of understanding.

▶ The development of language and the understanding of how to use it appropriately, thus extending the ability to reflect on the nuances of ideas and to express opinions with greater clarity and accuracy. This helps in the avoidance of vague, unsupported opinion and enhances a sharper focus of thought.

▶ The development of thinking for learning extends reasoning powers and cognitive skills—the ability to prioritize and structure thoughts, and to research and seek evidence, deepening a sense of understanding.

▶ Collaborative learning and talking are important, building on the social activity of dialogue to develop team skills, working within a role and enhancing the skills of listening and effective questioning.

▶ There is a role for parallel thinking, that is adopting different views of a problem. For example, using de Bono's (1999) "Six Hat Thinking", which moves beyond the conflict of opposing opinion to develop a more rounded approach to critical thinking by engaging in multiple viewpoints, which may enable us to step outside our natural predispositions.

▶ There is a complexity to thinking for learning in that the student may be aware both of the process and of the subject matter. The benefit of this approach is shown by classroom research in which two parallel groups of students were taught the same topic, one with the traditional transmission of information and the other through a thinking skills strategy. Later testing of knowledge and understanding reflected similar levels of retention, but the latter group were able to use the adopted thinking strategy in different contexts.

Reflection

What opportunities for developing thinking skills did you have as a student?

How might the range of thinking skills referred to be carried forward by lifelong learners?

Of the range of skills, which do you currently employ in your classroom/ school?

Are there particular training needs for staff in your school in relation to thinking for learning strategies?

Do the principles and characteristics of thinking for learning fit with the school's culture and ethos?

Can the processes and characteristics of thinking for learning be adapted to students of any age?

As Rockett and Percival (2002) state:

> It has become increasingly apparent that young people of any age can be taught to think more clearly, to express themselves and their thoughts more eloquently and to grow in self-esteem as a result. These attributes do not develop in all students simply through exposure to challenging and interesting tasks. Their thought processes and strategies for dealing with questions and problems need to be made explicit to them.

So what might a thinking for learning opportunity look like? According to Dewey (1916):

We can teach students what constitutes good thinking, but without that being motivated and disposed to engage in good thinking when the occasion arises, such instruction comes to naught.

It would seem axiomatic, therefore, that effective thinking for learning may be more effective in atmosphere-centred, positive relationships. Robert Swartz (1995), however, believes that thinking skills help to develop a positive attitude towards learning through engagement by using practical exercises that offer success for each student. Having established a motivation and predisposition for learning, the structure of a thinking-for-learning approach may be as outlined as below:

FRAMING	Begin by improving the big picture—setting the context for the challenge.
COGNITIVE CHALLENGE	Establishing the task, which needs to be sufficiently taxing, pushing the learner just beyond the zone of comfort.
MEDIATION	The teacher providing support and prompting through careful questioning of the processes of learning, but not providing a set of questions.
DEBRIEFING	Metacognition, talking about the thinking. This may take place throughout the process or at the end as an evaluation.
TRANSFER AND BRIDGING	How that thinking might be used in other situations—thus developing that necessary lifelong learning approach.

Having explored key principles, processes and structure it would seem appropriate to make reference to several examples of specific thinking for learning strategies. Limitations of space allow us to refer to only a small number of an expanding repertoire of thinking strategies (Figure 4.2).

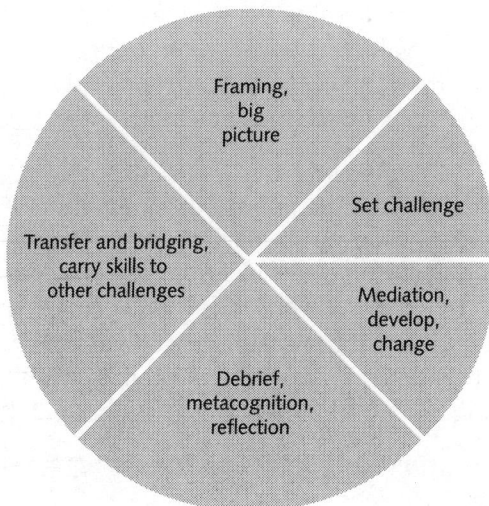

Figure 4.2: Thinking cycle

Strategies

Odd one out

This is a very simple strategy that can be used at any point to stimulate further discussion, provide opportunity for explanation and prompt a range of questioning.

Decide which of the following is the odd one out and for which reasons:

▶ Moscow, Atlanta, London, Athens

You may decide Atlanta because it is not a capital city. You may suggest Moscow as it is eastern European; Atlanta because it has seven letters and the others only have six, or because it is not a capital; London as it is the only one that is a future Olympics venue; or Athens as it is the birthplace of the Olympics.

This process encourages the skills of classification, justification and the awareness of a range of possible alternatives—there is no fixed right or wrong answer.

Try the following:

▶ horse, zebra, sheep, cow
▶ ferry, trawler, liner, yacht
▶ Liverpool, Real Madrid, Los Angeles Galaxy, Barcelona
▶ tennis, polo, athletics, cricket

Diamond ranking

This is a prioritizing strategy that develops setting and working with a range of criteria. It is a valuable strategy that enables students to develop the skills of evaluation and explanation, and to identify points of relevance and importance. Prioritizing is clearly a key skill for life and can help with time management, target setting and planning of extended writing.

Put nine pictures, statements, objects or words onto a set of cards so that they can be moved around. Working in pairs or groups, learners are asked to "rank" them in order of importance. The teacher may set a list of criteria, or as learners become more experienced they may wish to set a range of different criteria with an explanation for their choice. More than nine cards can be provided, to enable the learner to reject some and focus on the most relevant (Figure 4.3).

You may wish to prioritize what is shown in Figure 4.4 in terms of your personal training needs.

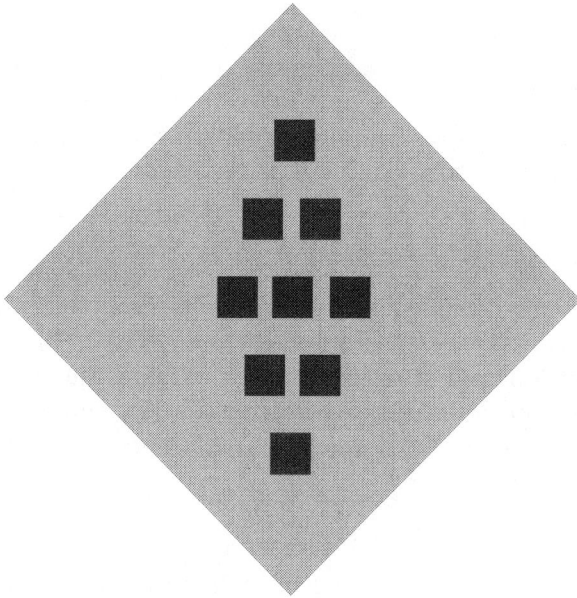

Figure 4.3: Diamond ranking

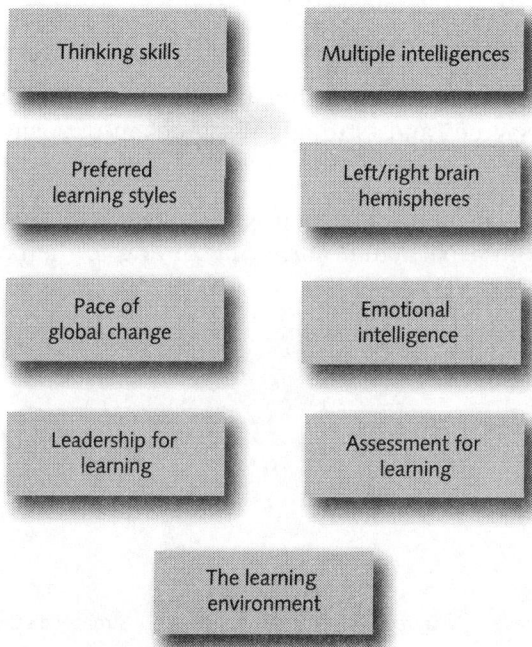

Figure 4.4: Training needs and priorities

The diamond ranking exercise may be used as an individual as well as a collaborative task. Such an approach may also be used as part of a self-review process, for example in the understanding of mathematical concepts. The group's diamond ranking results can then be analysed by the teacher to provide a set of priorities for revision prior to formal assessments.

Opinion lines/corners, concept lines

These are active strategies, meeting the needs of kinaesthetic learners, which help to develop speaking and listening skills. The process focuses on the development of negotiation, persuasion and clarification skills and the appreciation of diversity through recognizing differences of opinion. The opportunity for persuasion encourages the use of key language.

Why is this an important strategy?

Learners are actively involved in building their own understanding, helping to create a climate in which opinions are valued. The teacher acts as mediator, encouraging a focus on key language and ensuring that the tasks set are challenging and relevant to students. The process strongly supports speaking and listening skills, collaborative working and the recognition of diversity.

How is the process managed?

For opinion corners the teacher posts signs stating "strongly agree", "agree", "disagree" and "strongly disagree" in opposite corners of the room (Figure 4.5).

The learners are then provided with a statement and asked to place themselves in a particular corner according to their views. Learners

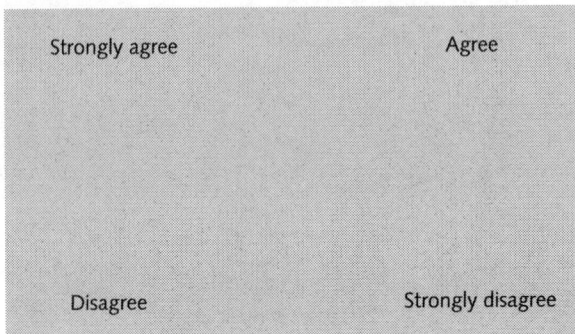

Figure 4.5: Opinion corners

are then asked to justify their opinions and may question each other; this frequently leads to a physical realignment as students listen to points of view and may be persuaded to change their positions. The given statement may be slightly ambiguous and learners may wish to question to seek clarification.

Concept lines, a similar exercise, may be used to introduce more subtle gradings of view. Whereas corners tend to accentuate differences and encourage explaining, reasoning and persuading skills, concept lines help to introduce skills of sorting and classifying, and encourage discussion about the properties of ideas.

Exercise with staff

Place the 12 statements shown in Figure 4.6 onto two sets of cards and ask two groups of staff to prioritize the cards in relation to what they believe to be important aspects of the learning process for their students. The cards should be kept hidden from the "opposing" group until the mediator asks the groups to lay them out in order of ascending priority. This exercise involves discussion, classifying, clarifying, and justifying both within and between groups; the authors have even witnessed the physical moving of colleagues to resolve differing views!

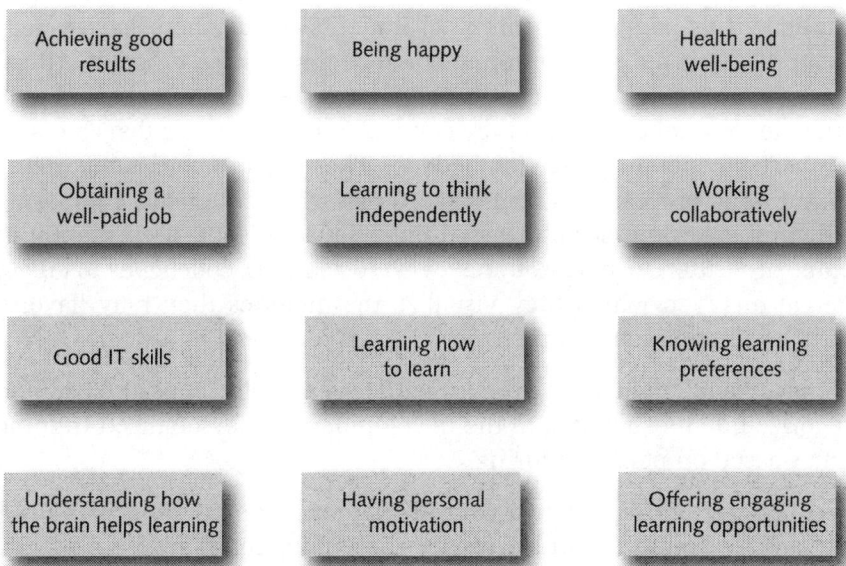

Achieving good results	Being happy	Health and well-being
Obtaining a well-paid job	Learning to think independently	Working collaboratively
Good IT skills	Learning how to learn	Knowing learning preferences
Understanding how the brain helps learning	Having personal motivation	Offering engaging learning opportunities

Figure 4.6: Twelve statement cards

You may wish to attempt this exercise with different school groups, staff, students and parents, and compare priorities. There are no right or wrong answers; rather, the exercise affords the opportunity to develop clarity of language and effective persuasive skills, which will hold anyone in good stead in our changing world.

You might also like to explore other thinking for learning strategies, such as "Mysteries", in which learners are provided with a range of statements and asked to act as detectives, classifying, ordering and structuring fragments of information in order to answer a given question or mystery. Such an approach deepens understanding, aids collaboration and develops questioning techniques beyond the transmission of information.

Other strategies that make effective use of visual stimulation to aid memory are thinking diagrams and thinking maps, the latter developed by David Hyerle (2004). These are eight fundamental thinking skills defined and animated by maps, providing a common visual language for thinking and learning across the whole school community. These strategies are based on an understanding that the brain is a pattern seeker and is dominantly visual. As Jensen and Johnson (1995) say, "90% of all information that comes into our brains is visual".

Thinking maps, therefore, act as both concrete pictures of abstract concepts and visual patterns for thinking. Students and teachers learn a clear visual process to aid their thinking when dealing with a range of critical or creative thinking tasks. The learners have a set of tools that may be applied to new concepts, and they can tackle new complex texts by "seeing" the concepts and ideas embedded. The maps enable categorizing and chunking processes to take place, assist with sequences, comparing conflicting ideas and structuring complex ideas prior to presentation in graphic or written format. You may wish to ask your colleagues to create a "circle map", in which they visualize the qualities they may have to offer to their students (Figure 4.7).

You may wish to repeat the exercise with several colleagues and begin to categorize qualities leading to the development of personalized training models based on peer mentoring.

Hyerle (2004) points out two central themes—"construction of knowledge" and "communities of learning"—as thinking maps are:

A transformative language for learning for personal growth, for collaborative work across complex and increasingly virtual technological organizations and societies, and as common pathways for communicating across diverse languages and cultures.

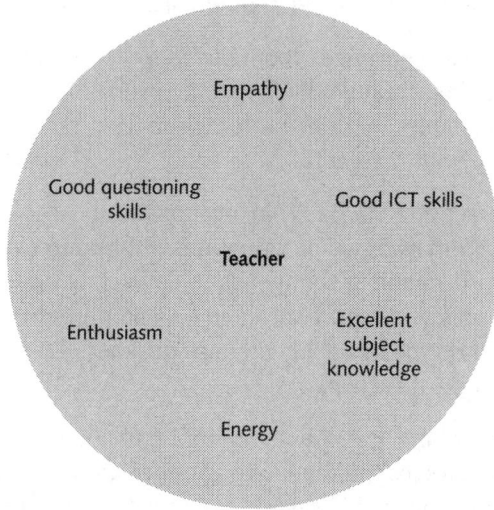

Figure 4.7: Circle map

In addition to the above exercise, the reader may wish to explore other approaches, such as the lateral thinking approach of Edward de Bono (1999). In the CoRT (Cognitive Research Trust) programme, students are encouraged to regularly practise the development of their thinking skills as an operating process to develop potential intelligence. This explicit accessing of thinking skills echoes the work of Art Costa's (2003) "habits of mind". He emphasizes the importance of being clear about what characterizes effective thinking and ensuring that such habits are infused into the learning process to improve effective decision-making.

CASE STUDY

Adrienne Jensen/Hiroshima International School/Japan

Constructing meaning using Six Hat Thinking

Teaching students using the inquiry process necessitates a variety of strategies that are effective, investigative and open-ended. Building confidence and developing a thriving enthusiasm requires a supportive and scaffolded environment that genuinely values risk-taking. Developing children to be lateral thinkers in this process requires using a range of learning strategies designed to promote thinking skills.

Piaget first suggested that children do not simply absorb knowledge passively, but need to actively construct meaning for themselves in order to learn. Using inquiry learning helps to develop attitudes of mind that are conducive to critical thinking. These attitudes include having an open mind, being fair-minded and having a critical, enquiring attitude.

Inquiry learning and its challenges should be designed to bring together inquiry skills, reasoning, creative thinking and evaluation. Six Hat Thinking (Edward de Bono) enables these higher-order thinking skills to be used in a quick and easy way with regularity.

The elements to practising Six Hat Thinking are strongly rooted in dialogue (as is the Primary Years programme), with group working being an important feature, enabling confidence to develop in oral skills and participation. The ability to report back and explain thoughts completes the main elements to this type of thinking. These qualities also focus students' attention on the kinds of thinking they use.

Each of de Bono's six hats describes a different thinking operation. Using the six thinking hats forces the thinker to consider the problem, question, stimulus material or challenge in several dimensions, and is effective in developing a fully rounded picture of an area or concept. It offers a structure for thinking and leads to greater confidence on the part of the learner.

Meaning-making is a constructive process—understanding requires a model from, or link to, our unique personal world. It is not individual—shared knowledge is constructed through the interconnections and coherence of diverging viewpoints. The activity of constructing meaning is what our brain stores.

Learning to think is enhanced when teachers make thinking skills explicit by labelling cognitive processes and habits of mind when they occur, employing thinking maps and diagrams, and modelling the steps of problem-solving, decision-making and investigating (Costa 2003).

Hats can be introduced one at a time, or altogether, and while there is no specific order in which the hats should be introduced, it is usually a good idea for younger students to start with the yellow hat as it develops a positive viewpoint.

Six Hat Thinking can be effectively used to make each of the learner profile characteristics known to students. A concept map-organizing format can be established, using a 'spoke' for each of the hats. The profile attribute is placed in the middle and the children are asked to use the hats to generate their ideas on what it looks, sounds and feels like.

For example, using the example of encouraging open-mindedness:

▶ White-hat thinking helps us to define the term—what it is.

▶ Yellow-hat thinking generates a list of positives about showing this characteristic.

▶ Green-hat thinking provides examples of how children can show their open-mindedness.

▶ Red-hat thinking links with how they will feel when they are being open-minded.

▶ Blue-hat thinking enables children to ask themselves how they could be open-minded more often, and why it is important. During this time they are reflecting on their own behaviour.

▶ Black-hat thinking demonstrates the clearness and fairness in using this in our community —it addresses the people we don't want to become.

▶ When the process is complete, children have a very rounded idea of the profile attribute and can see the benefits of displaying it.

Equally, Six Hat Thinking can be applied to discrete subject areas such as mathematics. When employed within a problem-solving process, it can be linked with Pólya's (1887–1985) four step process (See, Plan, Do, Check). For each step, children use the hats as prompts to aid thinking about the step they are employing. For example, white-hat thinking is used to find the information in the "See" stage, green-hat and black-hat thinking are used in the "planning" stage (What can I use? Would it work?) and blue-hat thinking is used in the "check" stage in their work.

Some other suggestions that regularly work in inquiry classrooms are:

▶ Begin a unit of work at the "What do we Know?" stage, and employ all of the hats to determine links and prior experience.

▶ During writing episodes, use green-hat and red-hat thinking for developing storylines and empathy, yellow-hat thinking for positive criticism from others, and blue-hat thinking for editing.

▶ Discussions about personal, social and emotional aspects can use all the hats for developing viewpoints about and looking at a situation.

▶ Encouraging active participation in reading circles is accomplished through Six Hat Thinking as students look for ways to improve their reading and encourage others through positive comments.

Six Hat Thinking is a most effective way to bring about self-evaluation at the end of a unit of work or for a summative assessment piece.

The broader aim of Six Hat Thinking is to promote metacognition—being conscious of our own thinking. By introducing a challenge or situation, then having students describe their plans and strategies for solving each problem, sharing their thinking along the way, and reflecting and evaluating the strategies they have used, children are learning about their own learning.

This is the very essence of what Jean Piaget was talking about. In working with students in this way, we are helping them to acquire the capacity to learn and change consciously, continually and quickly—attributes needed for 21st-century learners.

Finally, the work of Matthew Lipman (2003), who developed Philosophy for Children (P4C) can enable an exploration of the notion of questioning techniques. "Student reasonableness" is developed through encouraging children to think about moral and ethical issues that may interest them. Students participate in enquiry and talk in a managed, supportive manner, developing clarity of language and effective listening skills. Children as young as 4 or 5 years may be able to discuss the morality of a fairy story or traditional tale, for example debating when it may be appropriate not to tell the truth.

CASE STUDY

Lisa Grant/St Cecilia's Catholic Infant and Nursery School/Liverpool, UK

Philosophy for children

St Cecilia's Catholic Infant and Nursery School is a two-form entry school based in Tuebrook, a suburb in Liverpool. The school has 215 pupils aged between 3 and 7 years. The starting point at entry into nursery is well below national expectations.

Over five years ago, Philosophy for Children was introduced at St Cecilia's as part of a strategic plan to create a Thinking School. We wanted to encourage critical and creative thinking and to develop the skills that will assist the children in playing a full and active role in society.

Philosophy for Children advocates a methodology for encouraging pupils to think about moral and ethical issues that interest them, with the aim of encouraging reasonableness. It is not a study of the work of philosophers; it is an attempt to engage pupils in enquiry and discussion. In a supportive environment learners are encouraged to ask and respond to questions that they themselves have generated, and to think critically about opinions that they and others hold.

Children in Key Stage 1 (education system in England—curriculum covering ages 5–7) classes have a weekly philosophy lesson. The children all sit on chairs in a circle so that they are comfortable and can all see each other. The lesson usually starts with a mental warm-up, which will involve the children using both sides of their brain. The children are then introduced to a story read by the teacher. They are asked to discuss the story and come up with a philosophical question. These questions are written on the board exactly as the children have worded them. The children then have an omnivote, which means that they can vote for more than one question. In these lessons the teacher acts as the facilitator, not the leader. At the end of the discussion each child has the chance to make an unchallenged comment. Children in the foundation stage are introduced to the conventions of discussion and debate during Circle Time activities.

In St Cecilia's, Philosophy for Children has had a dramatic impact on raising self-esteem and intellectual confidence, improving listening and questioning skills, and promoting care and collaboration.

Methods of delivery

Having outlined a range of possible strategies, it is important to consider a method of delivery. Should this be taught through separate courses, identified clearly as additional to normal curriculum, to enhance the separate skills of thinking?

The advantages of the approach of a specific "learn to think" course are clearly to raise the profile of the skill of thinking, emphasizing the art of metacognition and highlighting the importance of developing the art of creative and critical thinking. Focus on aspects such as thinking maps and the development of a culture of the thinking school will provide both teacher and student with access to sets of learning tools that may be adapted for use across a range of learning situations.

Should the approach be one of subject-specific courses focusing on particular areas of the curriculum which lend themselves to relevant strategies, therefore explicitly subject related? Alternatively, would an infusion method be preferable, where the skills may be less explicitly clear but be an embedded part of learning delivery? An embedded approach can carry the advantage of increasing the relevance of particular thinking strategies in given learning situations and over time can become an embedded part of the learning process if replicated across curriculum areas.

Each of the previous approaches is of merit, and their use may depend upon the culture of the organization, the level of staff involvement and commitment, and the perceived value of particular strategies.

What can be seen, however, is that thinking for learning is a growing area of expertise. It is an area aligned to development in brain research, psychology and the philosophy of learning. The need for reflection, metacognition, language development and the enhancing of critical and creative thinking approaches has never been greater required in our complex, ever-changing world.

CHAPTER 5

Emotional intelligence

The headline of a UK newspaper, the *Independent on Sunday*, on 29 April 2007 proclaimed "Respect! Good manners to be taught in all schools".

The accompanying article, by Marie Wolff, the paper's political editor, reported that

> Children in secondary schools are to be taught "emotional intelligence" as part of the national curriculum in an attempt to combat a growing tide of rudeness, violence and lack of respect. With the debate about the lack of civility among young people reaching a new pitch, ministers are planning to roll out "social and emotional" intelligence classes to help children to cope with anger and frustration without resorting to violence and swearing.

Why has the UK government made this decision?

One reason might lie in an analysis advanced by Belinda Harris (2007):

> Schools are powerhouses of emotion as individuals engage with each other, with learning, with their values, and with the everyday pleasures, excitements and joy that occur when relationships and learning combine in creative exploration and discovery. They are also minefields of disappointment, envy, "fear, anguish, depression, humiliation, grief and guilt", and not just for the teachers involved. In Jeffrey and Woods' (1996) study of teacher stress it is clear that children and young people also bear the brunt of teachers' negative emotions in the "field" that is the classroom.

Daniel Goleman (1998) has an equally disturbing answer:

> As children grow ever smarter in IQ, their emotional intelligence is on the decline. Perhaps the most disturbing single piece of data comes from a massive survey of parents and teachers that shows the present generation of children to be more emotionally troubled than the last. On average, children are growing more lonely and depressed, more angry and unruly, more nervous and prone to worry, more impulsive and aggressive.

He proceeds to cite a disturbing litany of behaviours in young people that substantiate his assertions: alienation, drug abuse, crime and violence, depression (and now an increasing number of suicides), bullying and disaffection with the educational process. Clearly, the implications for the workforce of the future are very significant.

To follow this particular line of argument to a logical conclusion, Goleman uses an employers' survey of required competencies in new recruits to the workforce to show that the only academic requirements were in the areas of literacy and numeracy. All the others were in the domain of emotional intelligence, such as:

▶ the ability to listen
▶ the ability to communicate
▶ good interpersonal and intrapersonal skills
▶ self-confidence
▶ self-management (i.e. the ability to effectively manage one's own emotions, particularly the disruptive ones)
▶ empathy
▶ high levels of motivation
▶ good teamwork skills.

CASE STUDY

Colegio Olinca Cuernavaca/Mexico

Disciplinary model

Olinca's disciplinary model helps develop some traits of the IB learner profile among students, teachers and parents. This model stands on the following premises:

▶ The school's mission is to form better human beings.
▶ Any disciplinary conflict is a learning opportunity for students, teachers and parents.
▶ The objective is to help students become responsible for their actions and their consequences.

When a disciplinary conflict arises, the students involved speak about their actions and their motives. Each of them has the right to speak without interruptions and to be heard by a teacher with an open mind and heart. Using questions, the teacher helps each student reflect on his or her actions. As students speak and answer they learn to become good communicators: being able to describe a conflict, state a personal point of view and express a reflection entails self-knowledge and assertiveness. Finally, the teacher asks the students for possible solutions to the conflict or what the consequences of their actions should be. The teacher listens to them and decides which consequence will be applied. The consequence must be logical, fair and challenging as it helps students to continue reflecting and become principled.

This disciplinary model also promotes the recognition of academic, social or emotional accomplishments made by the students in a verbal or written form. As students are acknowledged, the teacher helps them reflect on their strengths and actions using the process described above.

There is a paradox behind these experiences: as teachers help students learn they become thinkers, inquirers, reflective, principled and good communicators. Olinca's disciplinary model is really helping all of us to become better human beings.

Few would disagree that in the last 20 years (and certainly the last 10) educators have accepted the notion of Gardner's (1993) "multiple intelligences" and that we should move to accommodate these in how we teach. As Stoll and Fink (1995) pointedly emphasize:

> *Perhaps more insidious for many students is the decontextualised nature of much of what students are expected to learn. Getting the correct answer is more important than understanding the concepts behind the problem.*

Gardner's (1993) concept of "multiple intelligences" has already been discussed in Chapter 3, but it is important to recognize that it leads to a much more democratic and inclusive concept of learning and intelligence. The challenge is not one of sorting the fit and the less fit but rather of developing all of these minds.

Stoll and Fink (1995) also refer to the work of Reich (1992), who maintains that in a postmodern world individuals will need the following skills if they wish to success:
- ▶ abstraction—the capacity for discovering patterns and meaning
- ▶ systems thinking—to see relationships among phenomena
- ▶ experimentation—the ability to find one's own way through continuous learning
- ▶ social skills to collaborate with others.

The challenge facing schools is to modify the education system to take account of the way people learn but also to help prepare students for the new types of workplaces that are emerging and the skills required for them.

Diane Schilling (1996) has provided probably the best synthesis of this challenge:

> *The brightest futures belong to students who develop EQ along with IQ and to school communities whose citizens have the courage to risk being human in the classroom, lunchroom, office, playground, workroom and playing field.*

Returning to Gardner—his *Multiple Intelligences: The Theory in Practice*, published in 1993, summarizes the personal intelligences:

> *Interpersonal intelligence is the ability to understand other people: what motivates them, how they work, how to work co-operatively with them. Successful salespeople, politicians, teachers, clinicians and religious leaders are all likely to be individuals with high degrees of interpersonal intelligence. Intrapersonal intelligence ... is a correlative ability, turned inward. It is a capacity to form an accurate, veridical model of oneself and to be able to use that model to operate effectively in life.*

In "Multiple Intelligences Go to School", Gardner and Hatch (1989) suggest that intrapersonal intelligence is the key to self-knowledge, which includes "access to one's own feelings and the ability to discriminate among them and draw upon them to guide behaviour".

So important have these intelligences become that Catherine Lewis (2004) maintains that:

> *A growing body of research indicates that social and emotional learning, in fact, lays a foundation for academic achievement. A comprehensive social and emotional learning programme, well grounded in research, can actually help a school ... reach its academic achievement goals.*

Social intelligence

At this stage it is important to appreciate that there are critics of the competing model of emotional intelligence and, indeed, Goleman (2006) has recognized this by introducing a new concept of social intelligence. He writes persuasively:

> *Here the picture enlarges beyond a one-person psychology—those capacities an individual has written—to a two-person psychology: what transpires as we connect.*

Harris (2007) moves the argument on even further:

more creative relationships are needed, founded on deep inner awareness, knowledge and understanding of self in all constructive and destructive configurations. In this way, the self that engages with students, colleagues, parents, governors and the wider educational community is fully present (emotionally, intellectually, spiritually and morally), fully inclusive ... (and ... able to reach out and "touch" the needs, wishes and preference of the other).

Much of this has been influenced by the nature of educational change, by what Harris (2007) calls "speaking", in particular the widespread understanding and development of the link between school leadership and school effectiveness. This has created many tensions in the educational community, not least of all because, as Fullan (2004) has pointed out many times, change is complex and, unless the process is understood, it often leads to frustration and failure. Again, as Harris (2007) articulates:

Concerns about the sustainability of school change highlight the importance of engaging with the emotional undertone of the staffroom and classroom ... Such emotional and intellectual integrity helps to sustain the momentum of change.

Reflection

You might like to reflect on the concept of change through the following exercise. Select an element of change you have experienced in the past couple of years:

▶ How was the change introduced?
▶ What pressure was there to introduce it?
▶ What was the level of support for the change?
▶ What was the time factor?
▶ Did the change process focus on task or on people?
▶ How did you feel about the process?
▶ What (if anything) would have improved the process?

This reflective exercise is not merely designed to examine the nature of the change process, it is also designed to probe the degree of stress that often underpins such change. It is indisputable that in many state schools, in both the USA and the UK, there is considerable pressure on teachers to maximize their students' results. Confronted with this, plus the added pressure of disaffected students, it is little wonder that teaching becomes very teacher directed, with little time allowed for the personalized learning agenda or, indeed, the acquisition of independent learning techniques. It is also unsurprising that the education market is suddenly awash with books and manuals on behaviour management. Of course, the greater the focus on the teacher, the greater the stress. In many cities around the world, increasingly large numbers of students are disaffected and suffer from neglect and abuse. Continually being confronted with test regimes will not endear students to the learning process, nor will it provide them with the degree of emotional intelligence required to cope with their distress. On the other hand, teachers have received little or no training in this area and therefore look (understandably) for an instant solution. Many governments completely fail to see the inherent dichotomy in the demand to improve results coupled with the demand that schools are inclusive. These competing demands are explosive, and much of the challenge for school leaders today is to create opportunities for teachers to engage with issues surrounding emotional and social intelligence as well as attempting to move the school towards "more attentive, attuned, accepting, affirming and appreciative relationships" (Harris 2007).

In the UK the attainment agenda has also seen a corresponding rise in the number of expulsions, increased teacher turnover, increased difficulties in recruiting headteachers and increased violence—both student-on-student and, less often, student-on-teacher. The micro-management of schools through target-driven objectives has rankled with teachers, who feel that their professional discretion has been curtailed and has created barriers to resolving many of the above concerns. Essentially, they have lost the "locus of control": the extent to which the individual can influence his or her life and work.

Distributed leadership is coming to be seen as an important element in supporting teachers in regaining an element of the locus of control inside the classroom and perhaps breaking what, for many, is a negative emotional cycle. Many teachers are beginning to seek out a new approach to engaging with young people. However, as Harris (2007) is quick to point out, distributed leadership is not merely about areas of responsibility; it is also about the "emotional domain" and the need to ensure that the emotional workload is evenly distributed and to appreciate the emotional dimension to the change process.

Fullan (2004) has identified a number of factors relating to the change process that clearly have an "emotional" dimension to them:

▶ Behaviour changes before beliefs/attitudes.
▶ Successful management is not about one's own success, but about fostering success in others.
▶ The goal is to develop individuals, who in turn improve the organization.

▶ Shared vision and ownership is as much an outcome of a quality process as it is a precondition.

▶ Assume that conflict and disagreement are not only inevitable but fundamental to successful change—any group of people possesses multiple realities, any collective change attempt will necessarily involve conflict.

At the heart of this is the concept of culture—in changing or transforming any organization it is necessary to change its culture. Because culture is largely implicit and will certainly encompass habits and attitudes that affect the whole organization, it is not easy to define. Moreover, it will also encompass the mini-cultures of departmental and pastoral teams. It must, however, have the capacity to engage in what have often been referred to as "fierce conversations", whereby individuals and groups can challenge one another in a climate of trust in which the collaborative "we work together on this" supersedes the "I" and "it" culture that exists in many schools. Notwithstanding this, it is essential that all staff (and ideally all children) come to accept responsibility for their own lives, and their own emotions and feelings. This is a message that is forcibly delivered in many publications, from Goleman through to self-help flyers, such as that which appeared in the *Independent* newspaper in 2006: "40 ways to improve your emotional intelligence".

This particular flyer is interesting, not only because it reinforces the message of accountability, but also because it is strong on accentuating the positive. Among the 40 ways listed are the following:

▶ Stand tall: your physical posture can have a big effect on how you feel.

▶ Centre yourself: paying attention to your centre makes you feel stronger.

▶ Anchor your good feelings: remember a time when you felt really good and in control. Practise getting into those good feelings until these are "anchored".

▶ Deal with your inner critic.

▶ Challenge negative self-talk.

▶ Seek "win/win" outcomes: in negotiations and situations of potential conflict, remember that the agreements that work best are those that work for all concerned.

▶ Focus on what you want, not what you don't want: you tend to get what you focus on.

These points are particularly important because they underpin the fact that:

> *Good teaching and positive emotion go hand in hand.*
>
> *(Harris 2007)*

Hargreaves (2001) eloquently reinforces this view:

> *As an emotional practice teaching activates, colours and expresses the feelings and action of teachers and those they influence. All teaching is therefore inextricably emotional, either by design or default. Teachers can enthuse their students or bore them.*

Teachers who are relaxed, positive about their job and "destressed", and who feel that the locus of control lies with them, are in a far better position to be good teachers, are "fit for purpose" and therefore are less likely to underperform. The obverse side of the case is equally clear—the greater the pressure, the greater the disaffection and the almost guaranteed certainty of reduced effectiveness in the classroom and in the school generally. Harris (2007) is particularly strong in this area:

> *It falls upon those in formal leadership roles to generate the energy and will necessary to engage in and effect school change*

and

> *Raising self esteem, developing community, restoring hope and building morale are inter-related facets of this process [of change and reform].*

Returning to the themes of disaffection, isolation, depression and abuse in young people, it is clear that only an emotionally healthy workforce will have the capacity to deal with these issues.

Engaging with students in the realm of emotional intelligence is now an absolute requirement—the task of school leadership is to create the conditions that promote individual growth, develop positive cultural norms in the school, create a strong sense of community and mitigate some of the more stressful elements of change.

Getting students to think about their emotions from a "secure base" (i.e. one which provides the requisite levels of support and care) now needs to be considered a priority for most schools, whatever their circumstances.

The following are some suggestions that could provide opportunities for just such an exploration.

Strategy

Learned optimism

This was the title of a book by Martin Seligman, published in 1991. In it he suggests that:

> *Learning how to think more optimistically when we fail gives us a permanent skill for warding off depression. It can also help us achieve more and have better health.*

This is a rich discussion topic for staff and students alike.

Distribute pictures of Eeyore and Tigger from A A Milne's series of *Winnie the Pooh* books to the group. In general terms, explore what sort of emotions might be associated with each of the characters.

This will provide an opportunity for exploring issues around the concepts of optimism and pessimism. Once the group has discussed the two characters, put up the following charts:

When GOOD things happen	
Optimistic	**Pessimistic**
Personal—I make good things happen	External—I didn't have much to do with it
Permanent—things will be great forever	Temporary—it was a blip
Pervasive—it will spill over into everything I do	Isolated—I won't change anything else

When BAD things happen	
Optimistic	**Pessimistic**
External—I didn't have much to do with it	Personal—I make bad things happen
Temporary—it was a blip	Permanent—things will be awful forever
Isolated—it won't change anything else. It's unusual for this to happen to me	Pervasive—my whole life will be ruined. It always happens to me

This discussion will easily lead to concepts such as self-esteem, self-efficacy and self-talk.

Self-esteem

Self-esteem has been defined as "the disposition to experience oneself as competent to cope with the basic challenges of life and worthy of happiness" (Branden 1994). With high self-esteem comes a strong sense of purpose and self-acceptance; with low self-esteem comes self-destructive behaviour such as apathy, isolation, depression, hostility and often substance abuse. It follows, therefore, that self-efficacy is "your own estimation of your ability to cause, bring about, or make happen those things that are important to you. It's your confidence in your ability to learn, make good decisions, and think effectively".

CASE STUDY

DR HALA SHEKEN/AHLIYYAH SCHOOL FOR GIRLS/AMMAN, JORDAN

Counselling department success story

Believing in a student and building on his or her strengths changes the "I can't" into "I can".

Maya is a ninth grade student who has been offered an individual support teacher since she was in fifth grade, to no concrete benefit. At home she has a critically demanding mother and a warm but absent father. Being an only child, she was spoiled and catered for in a manner that fostered dependence, helplessness, lack of motivation and hatred towards school. Maya's teachers believed she lacks abilities in comprehension, reflection and understanding of major concepts. Maya's situation, in spite of continued class support, has been worsening, to a point that teachers were hopeless too.

This year, Dina, her new support teacher, worked hard at establishing a very cooperative relationship with her. Her main goal was to improve upon Maya's self-concept first, then academics would follow. Her genuine approach and refusal to give up on Maya, her long encouragement sessions with her, and her belief that all resources in school should be used made a huge difference.

Dina briefed the counsellor, who in turn studied her file and arranged for a three-way meeting. The counsellor witnessed a very strong rapport between Dina and Maya, and aimed at hearing Maya's own story. When asked "What exceptional times do you enjoy school and work?", she replied that it was when she worked on the school website during computer class. That question uncovered a strength that can be utilized to motivate her and allow her to feel successful. Upon showing interest in her computer skills, she revealed for the first time that she has her own website that she herself had programmed. It was something to be proud of. The amazement, appreciation and recognition she heard from both counsellor and Dina was unprecedented. Further on, her strength could be built upon, and a suggestion to use interactive maths programs that were available in the maths department was a fascinating idea to her. Two days later, Maya got her first-ever high grade in Arabic literature—a first-time proof that "I can" is a success story to build on. Maya continues to attend weekly counselling sessions—she makes herself visible by eye contact, a big smile and a straightened-up back and head. She reported feeling happy about school and she listens in class, asks when she doesn't understand, and requests a make-up exam when she is not satisfied with her grade.

Appreciation, genuine belief, validation, focus on strengths, a solution-focused brief therapy approach and creating opportunities for experiencing success can turn "I can't" into "I can".

Self-efficacy

In Albert Bandura's (1986) book, *Social Foundations of Thought and Action: A Social Cognitive Theory*, the characteristics of people with strong and weak self-efficacy are described.

Those with strong self-efficacy:
▶ approach difficult tasks as challenges rather than as threats
▶ set challenging goals and sustain strong commitment to them
▶ direct their analytical thinking at the task in order to perform most effectively
▶ attribute failures to insufficient effort or unfavourable conditions
▶ heighten effort in the face of difficulties and setbacks
▶ quickly recover their sense of efficacy after failures or setbacks
▶ are fairly resistant to stress and depression.

People with weak self-efficacy:
▶ shy away from difficult tasks and see them as threats
▶ have low aspirations and weak commitment to the goals they choose
▶ direct their analytical thinking at themselves, thereby disrupting performance
▶ dwell on personal deficiencies, obstacles and adverse outcomes
▶ attribute failure to their own deficiencies
▶ slacken their efforts or give up quickly in the face of difficulty

▶ are slow to recover their sense of efficacy after failure or setbacks

▶ are susceptible to excessive stress and depression.

Building high self-efficacy in schools is incredibly important, and teachers who understand the importance of high self-efficacy and self-esteem and know how to build these qualities in students are an extremely valuable resource. Schools and teachers can support such a "building programme" by applying Bandura's sources of self-efficacy. He outlines four such sources.

1 Mastering experiences

Successes build a robust belief in personal efficacy. Failure undermines it. Schools need to encourage persistent effort and create a self-sustaining cycle of success breeding further success.

2 Vicarious experiences

Showing students role models similar to themselves who have succeeded helps build students' belief in their own ability to do likewise.

3 Social persuasion

Social persuasion raises the belief that students have what it takes to succeed. The school structures activities that promote success in a variety of different ways.

4 Physical and emotional status

Efficacy is raised by improving physical state (using programmes such as Healthy Schools/Fitness for All—UK initiatives for developing health and fitness) and reducing stress (the HeartMath initiative). Perceived efficacy can be strengthened by a positive mood or weakened by a despondent mood.

The flip-side of this statement, however, is very quickly demonstrated by Goleman (1996):

> *People who cannot marshal some control over their emotional life fight inner battles that sabotage their ability for focused work and clear thought.*

The challenge for many schools is to give students the tools to manage their own emotions.

Self-talk

Introducing students to the concept of "self-talk", which is completely intertwined with self-esteem and self-efficacy, will begin to allow them to appreciate how behaviours, beliefs and emotional responses to events and experiences are substantially influenced by either positive or negative self-talk.

> **Reflection**
>
> Either do this short exercise yourself or ask your students to do it.
> ▶ What beliefs do you hold about yourself?
> ▶ Do you feel comfortable receiving genuine compliments? Why? If not, why not?
> ▶ Do you ever use "put-downs" on friends or family? If so, why? What sort of effect is that likely to have on them?
> ▶ What examples can you give of times when you have thought and talked negatively about yourself, at home or in school?
> ▶ What do you do when you hear negative talk?
> ▶ What might you do in the future?
> ▶ What are some of the ways you praise and encourage people?

Lou Tice (1997) states in his book *Personal Coaching for Results*:

> *If you were treated with respect and affection and saw those around you dealing optimistically and positively with life's challenges, your self-talk was probably positive. If you were constantly criticised, put down, and saw others blaming, worrying, and expect the worst, your self-talk more than likely mirrored those negative attitudes.*

The corollary to this, of course, is that by taking responsibility for your emotions and feelings, by becoming accountable, you then have a choice—you can move from a feeling of powerlessness to actually taking control of your feelings. This is a very important life skill.

Strategy

Comfort zones

Divide the group into pairs. Ask them to silently observe each other in terms of dress, looks and accessories. Then ask each pair to stand back-to-back and change two to three things about their appearance. Once completed, ask the pairs to face each other once again and point out the changes. Repeat the exercise either once or twice more. Then ask the group how they felt in the first minute or so—for example, what their levels of discomfort were. Then explore the challenge of changing things—explore the notion of how people can look (smiling, frowning, etc.) and how it might have been more difficult as the exercise was repeated.

Talk about the concept of comfort zones, where individuals or groups feel they can belong without fear of discomfort. Explore some of the physical symptoms we experience when we are outside our comfort zones. For example:

▶ greater difficulty in breathing
▶ tightening of the shoulder and neck muscles
▶ increased perspiration
▶ difficulty in speaking.

Ask the group to consider when comfort zones are good (safety in numbers or walking on well-lit streets, for example) and when it is a good thing to move out of a comfort zone (to challenge oneself, to explore new opportunities, and so on). Other tasks might be to ask students to draw concentric circles, where their comfort zone is the middle circle and their panic zone is the outside circle, and ask them to list, from the middle outwards, what activities they are most comfortable with and what would cause them panic.

This strategy can be the starting point for really getting students to think about what they are currently dissatisfied with and what aspects of their life they would like to change. And, of course, to examine what they are pleased with and what techniques or strategies they might use to make changes.

Emotional competency

The concepts of optimism, self-efficacy, self-esteem, positive self-talk and understanding comfort zones are designed to create in individuals an emotional competency in how we manage ourselves. This also leads to social competency in terms of how we handle relationships. In *Emotional Intelligence and Working with Emotional Intelligence,* Goleman (2004) summarizes these in two tables.

Personal competence: These competencies determine how we manage ourselves.

Self-awareness
Knowing one's internal states, preferences, resources and intuitions

Emotional awareness	Recognizing one's emotions and their effects
Accurate self-assessment	Knowing one's strengths and limits
Self-confidence	A strong sense of one's self-worth and capabilities

Self regulations

Managing one's internal states, impulses and resources

Self-control	Keeping disruptive emotions and impulses in check
Trustworthiness	Maintaining standards of honesty and integrity
Conscientiousness	Taking responsibility for personal performance
Adaptability	Flexibility in handling change
Innovation	Being comfortable with novel ideas, approaches and new information

Motivation

Emotional tendencies that guide or facilitate reaching goals

Achievement drive	Striving to improve or meet a standard of excellence
Commitment	Aligning with the goals of the group or organization
Initiative	Readiness to act on opportunities
Optimism	Persistence in pursuing goals despite obstacles and setbacks

Social competence: These competencies determine how we handle relationships.

Empathy

Awareness of others' feelings, needs and concerns

Understanding others	Sensing others' feelings and perspectives, and taking an active interest in their concerns
Developing others	Sensing others' development needs and bolstering their abilities
Services orientation	Anticipating, recognizing and meeting people's needs
Leveraging diversity	Cultivating opportunities through different kinds of people
Political awareness	Reading a group's emotional currents and power relationships

Social skills

Adeptness at inducing a desirable response in others

Influence	Wielding effective tactics for persuasion
Communication	Listing openly and sending convincing messages
Conflict management	Negotiating and resolving disagreements
Leadership	Inspiring and guiding individuals and groups
Change catalyst	Initiating or managing change
Building bonds	Nurturing instrumental relationships
Collaboration and cooperation	Working with others towards shared goals
Team capabilities	Creating group synergy in pursuing collective goals

The body of literature that focuses on emotional intelligence and emotional leadership, and their impact on our schools, is growing by the day. In *Leadership for Mortals* (2005), Dean Fink notes that:

> to create an environment in which teachers find "flow" requires
> leaders with emotional understanding. Such leaders learn to
> read the emotional responses of those around them and create
> emotional bonds with and among those with whom they interact.

Boyatzis's theory of self-directed learning is increasingly used as a model to underpin the evolution of emotionally intelligent leaders. Boyatzis identifies five steps, or discoveries, in this model.

1 My ideal self. (Who do I want to be?)
2 My real self. (Who am I, and what are my strengths and gaps?)
3 My learning agenda. (How can I build on my strengths while reducing my gaps?)
4 Experimenting with practising new behaviours, thoughts and feelings to the point of mastery.
5 Developing supportive and trusting relationships that make change possible.

Emotional intelligence starts at the top and must then filter its way down until there is a critical mass of people, including students, to create an "emotionally literate school" (Harris 2007).

CASE STUDY

BROADGREEN HIGH SCHOOL/LIVERPOOL, UK

Empathy the Broadgreen way

Over the past two years Broadgreen has developed a course taught by all group tutors, entitled "Learning to Learn", during which students are exposed to a variety of experiences focusing on the skills they need to acquire in order to learn. Teachers have been supported in this endeavour by the publication of a range of materials that are designed to stimulate student imagination and discussion. These materials are entitled "Learning at Broadgreen" and this particular example concentrates on empathy and why it is important to develop this particular quality or skill.

The attribute	What it feels like in the classroom or around school	What it looks like in the classroom or around school
Empathy		
We can show empathy by:	you feel safe in the yard because there are lots of teachers and you know they will protect you	we are more understanding of illnesses and disabilities
listening to and understanding other people's needs, and ...	when the lessons are fun instead of boring it sticks in your head and you remember it more	you can learn things from the posters on display
making sure people get extra help if they are behind in their work	to some pupils it may make them feel comfortable	our school is clean and safe
caring and sharing and making people feel like they are special	people get help when they need it	we look after people who are on their own
looking out for people when they need help	we have things like hoists for disabled pupils by the pool to help them swim	we have ramps for the disabled pupils
relating to other people's problems	you feel safe, because if you are hurt or need any help there is the medical room	the teachers understand everyone and their needs
helping others make new friends	it feels good because you can make friends very easily	we have sympathy for people who may be feeling low
guiding people in the right direction	you feel safe and protected by adults	you don't interrupt people while they are speaking, you put your hand up and listen to what they are saying
understanding each other's needs	we all play together and no-one feels different	you don't push past people on corridors, you hold the doors

The attribute	What it feels like in the classroom or around school	What it looks like in the classroom or around school
comforting people when they're upset	teachers could ask for our opinions on things	someone will always stop to help you if you need it
being friendly	we have good wheelchair facilities	people walk in the corridors and don't push people
being kind	we have translators in school to help kids who are new in the country	we respect our classrooms
opening doors for people	joining after-school clubs helps you understand each other	people who are stuck with their work get help
telling a teacher if someone is being bullied	the school has good disabled facilities	you don't give cheek to teachers because they're there to help you
helping people if they are struggling to do something	I feel safe in this school because there are lots of teachers to help you and your friends. If anyone gets hurt in the yard there are teachers about to help you	
learning sign language so that you can communicate with deaf pupils	when the teacher is in the yard you can tell them what the matter is and they can sort it out—that's really good	
making sure everyone gets involved	in our school we have deaf and disabled pupils and we have lifts to help them	

The attribute	What it feels like in the classroom or around school	What it looks like in the classroom or around school
putting yourself in someone else's place	it feels safe, especially in the science rooms when we do practicals which are fun—there is an emergency stop button so it's very safe	
helping people	there is a caretaker on duty at the gates to stop intruders coming in	
respecting others	the school is calm and we try to understand one another	
being polite and helping others	I feel protected and don't worry about not coping	
paying attention to other people's ideas		
putting ourselves in other people's shoes		

CHAPTER 6

Developing the learning environment

Do not confine your children to your own learning.
For they have been born in another time.

Hebrew proverb

Life for students is changing more rapidly now than at any other time in the development of mankind. Through neurological research we can explore the influence of the brain on the learning process and this developing understanding of the individuality of the learner is reinforced through increasing understanding of the impact of emotional intelligence and motivation. Our students are digital natives, making friends around the world through instant communication and open to the impact of global news every minute of the day. Despite all of these changes, would our classroom of today look significantly different to a time traveller from the early 20th century? The likelihood is that we would have a similar number of students, grouped as they would have been around furniture that has barely changed, and with one adult leading the learning process.

We do not all have the opportunity to demolish our school buildings and begin again, but we may be able to make our students' learning more individually meaningful by increasing our awareness of the significance of the physical environment around us. To make the fullest use of our increasing understanding of the variety of learning processes it would seem appropriate to seek ways of ensuring that our learning spaces complement and enhance that process rather than become limits and barriers to progress.

Key questions

To what extent do the classrooms we teach in differ from those when we were students?

How does the furniture and layout of the room enhance opportunities for the kinaesthetic learner?

Are rooms flexible enough to meet the needs of different learning strategies?

How have our learning environments been adapted to incorporate effective use of new technologies?

To what extent do colour, light, air quality and design enhance learning in these rooms?

To what extent are our school buildings inspirational for learning—making the best use of new technologies to motivate students?

> *We spend a lot of time trying to change people. The thing to do is to change the environment and people will change themselves.*
>
> *(Watson 2007)*

Changing our learning environment

Traditional teaching methods in unchanging environments served education systems well for many years; however, as our students change and we increasingly recognize their diversity, there is a need to search for more appropriate methods of developing lifelong learning skills.

CASE STUDY

Hanan Khalil/Ahliyyah School for Girls/Amman, Jordan

Visual Arts

Art in general is a world where one naturally becomes an open-minded inquirer, after letting go of all inhibitions, knowing and believing that each person is a creative soul.

The students, as well as the teachers, in my school are very much encouraged to pursue creativity with no boundaries. There is ample space to explore, appreciate and reflect.

There are many examples where the students have benefited and learned. One which is worth mentioning is when I was given the opportunity to take the girls to Turkey to see and explore the world of art in a modern and historical aspect. Spending those 10 days together was a great thing for us to establish that caring relationship; walking the streets and exploring in strange corners made them feel like independent risk-takers.

I asked my students for two assignments—one was to make an artwork about Turkey in general, as a place that comprises east and west, modern and old. I also assigned each student to look into patterns and textures—

this way I felt that I could have them focus on the general as well as the detailed. On returning to our country the students started the work—the photos which they took of the beautiful mosques and the landscapes or those from the modern art museums were looked upon to analyse and make use of. Each girl had a unique approach but they were mainly focusing on the contrast that they so clearly witnessed in that beautiful country.

An exhibition was held at the end of the year, showing their personal hands-on experience.

My approach is mainly to bombard my students with as much as I can, proving that there are no boundaries. I focus on the detail even when it comes to cleaning your brush, making art from original materials and getting inspiration from anywhere or anything.

The school is in a rich area in Jordan—even walks downtown are a rich experience for the girls; they search, research and learn to appreciate, and most importantly they understand that art is a universal language.

The art department (middle school)

A unique aspect that takes place in art classes and enhances learning is the freedom of movement that we allow for continuous collaboration and interaction. Students are given the liberty to move around and view their classmates' work, which enables them to exchange ideas and skills. Since the exchange of experiences to advance in art is indispensable, discussions on students' work are held among students and between them and the teacher, to create constructive criticism that is useful to both the students and their teacher. In the course of the work, the library and the Internet are constantly visited during classes for further research purposes on works of art and art techniques.

Moreover, students are taken to visit exhibitions to develop their artistic appreciation.

We believe that our strategy is related to the IB learner profile in that it helps develop inquirers, thinkers, communicators and principled, open-minded, caring and reflective risk-takers.

Barbara Prashnig (1998), in her book *The Power of Diversity*, refers to several fallacies about the learning process that still appear to persist in spite of developing understanding through a range of research methodologies. The first fallacy is that children learn best when seated upright at a desk or table, when in fact research indicates that, although some students learn best this way, many learn more effectively where a less formal design meets student differences. Thus, a simple method of rearranging furniture can immediately impact on group dynamics and student motivation. Where possible, a horseshoe shape of seating eliminates the back row isolation of some students and increases the teacher's zone of focus, which is usually 90% on those immediately in front of them.

A second fallacy is that students learn best in well-illuminated areas and damage their eyes if attempting to work in low light. In actual fact, we need twice as much light to read when aged 40 as when aged 20 and twice as much again by the age of 60. Bright, artificial light can make students hyperactive and has an adverse effect on the immune system. Concentration levels will be seen to improve in lower-lit areas, and the use of natural light is far more conducive to effective learning.

Hollwich (1979), who studied the impact of artificial cool-white (non-full-spectrum) lighting, found an increase in cortisol in people under such conditions, reflecting additional stress levels. Technology now enables the manufacture of natural full-spectrum fluorescent light bulbs, which give a feeling of natural daylight illumination, reducing fatigue, glare and eye strain. The reduction in fluorescent lighting also has a positive impact on students affected by the Irlen syndrome, which affects pattern recognition and reading development.

A further fallacy relates to the use of colour in classrooms, suggesting that any colour will do as long as it is cream or off-white. Significant research has taken place into the influence of colour and texture on the individual learning process. Colours often evoke a cultural style and can also have historic and symbolic references. In the 1970s, Birren (1979) reported that warm colours and brilliant lighting led to increased muscular tension, while distracting colour combinations can confuse the learner and slow reaction. The use of colour clearly varies according to the use of space, with perhaps the use of bright, welcoming colours in open, public spaces with more muted tones in learning areas, especially where computers are being used.

The effect of colour may also vary according to student ages, with red, orange and yellow being stimulating in young children, while adolescents appear to respond better to blues and greens.

In exploring the use of colour it is also important to ensure, where feasible, that furniture is considered, to avoid an institutional feeling in public areas and reinforce a welcoming and focused atmosphere. Research by Sinofsky and Knirck (1981) indicates that colour can influence students' attitudes, behaviour and learning outcomes. This is one area of learning environments that is relatively inexpensive to experiment with and change, perhaps through consultation with students, thus enhancing their involvement in the shaping of the learning environment.

An increasing awareness of the learning process and the opportunity to shape learning to the changing needs of the 21st century does set challenges for architects, designers and educationalists in envisaging new school buildings. This imagining of a new world of learning is taking shape across the globe, driven by a range of local, environmental aspects, and also by visionary organizations such as the Aga Khan Foundation and the United World Colleges. In Japan, for example, the designs of the Yuyu-no-mori Nursery School and Day Nursery focus on the importance of the shapes visible in the local environment, with a range of trees and shrubs planted to encourage environmental learning from the earliest ages. This key design factor, together with innovative approaches to play via large nets and cave spaces, provides a modern, innovative child-centred space with indirect lighting and natural ventilation.

In Singapore, the School of Art, Design and Media, with students at the other end of the age spectrum, is a building that symbolizes its curriculum, representing uniqueness and creativity. Challenging traditional teaching spaces in linear form, the building adopts a more flexible use of different-shaped spaces, merging indoor and outdoor, and enabling learning and interaction to flow throughout the building.

In India, the Vidyalankar Institute of Technology makes use of asymmetric spaces and recycled materials. Challenging the traditional space assumptions, teachers, students and designers create a more flexible use of space with an emphasis on increased human interaction.

A review of the Aga Khan Foundation Awards for school architecture reveals how the vision and commitment of a single individual can drive forward life-enhancing educational opportunities. The 2005 winner, Dièbèdo Francis Kèrè, was the first person from his village of Gando, in Burkina Faso, to study abroad. Subsequently, by fundraising and training local villagers, he constructed a school in his village using local, sustainable materials. The design makes best use of climatic conditions, allowing cool air to move through shaded areas. This school is a fine example of using practical design and materials, with full community involvement and the development of real lifelong learning building skills. The school may be seen as an embodiment of form and function and shows what can be achieved with vision and commitment.

In England a long-term programme is in place to redesign secondary school learning environments. The "Building Schools for the Future" programme provides an opportunity to reshape not only the learning environment but also the school day, the role of teachers and the curriculum and assessment offered to students. Schools need, therefore, to seek best practice from around the world in order to transform the learning environment to meet 21st-century challenges in an environmentally sustainable manner. To this end some schools in Liverpool are working with the education designer Scott Prisco, of the Prisco Group in New Jersey, USA. As the person responsible for the High School of the Future in Philadelphia in the USA, he has had the opportunity to work with educationalists, students and parents to meet the challenges of 21st-century lifelong learning.

CASE STUDY

Scott Prisco

Designing the High School of the Future

As an architect, designing the School of the Future in cooperation with the Microsoft Corporation and the Philadelphia School District was a dream come true. This was a "once in a lifetime" opportunity. The people from Microsoft (Mary Cullinane, Technology Architect) and the District (Ellen Savitz, Chief Development Officer) were looking for the latest, most exciting new ideas possible, with great expectations. However, there were other entities and considerations that continually reined in the project. Typically, as with all public projects, great ideas must be tempered to an affordable solution. In addition, the Philadelphia School Improvement Team (the entity coordinating all of their construction projects) recently completed a 200-page document that was issued to all architects as the "Bible" of standards to follow for all new design and construction projects. Needless to say, there was a huge disconnect between the idea of "standards" and that of "out of the box thinking". We had many meetings with the entire team, which required compromises. However, we had many design charrettes that involved every aspect of the project, from bricks to technology, and all aspects of the delivery of curriculum. Fortunately, Mary, Ellen, Mayia Entcheva (our chief designer) and myself had strong design suggestions that were victorious on many of the key design features during these meetings.

From the very inception of this project Microsoft created a theme that was present well before the architect was brought on board. Everything would have to be "continuous" (where learning is not dependent on time and place); "relevant" (where content, curriculum and tools are current and relevant); and "adaptive" (where instruction adapts to the needs of the individual student).

The one aspect of the design we all agreed upon was the necessity to create a "wow" factor for the students—to create a "cool" environment that they could and would respect. Our building, which has a white masonry façade, is located in a deprived neighbourhood of west Philadelphia. There are no instances of spray paint or vandalism anywhere. From the moment they walk up to the building and through the spaces, the students are excited to be there. Even during a recent tour of the facility I saw students working on a project there at 8.00 p.m.

The corridors have been designed as "streets" (much wider than a typical corridor), with large-vision panels looking into every space so you can experience the moment from inside the learning spaces or within the street. The finishes include pigmented concrete, exterior light fixtures, benches, tables, chairs and plenty of natural daylight. The street also serves as a learning environment and a social hub.

The café, which is completely open to the street, has a serving area and seating area, similar to a food court in a mall. Other considerations were to make all of the community spaces accessible from the ground level, including the gymnasiums, fitness centre, performing arts areas, cafeteria, interactive learning centre and administration. An important part of the design process was to include the community. We had many interactive meetings with parents and various local church groups.

Flexibility and adaptability was one of the key components of the classroom learning environments. The spaces include moveable walls (sound rating equivalent to a 15 cm block wall), small group instruction rooms and furniture (tables and chairs) on castors. The rooms are constantly changing configuration to accommodate each specific lesson plan. Science labs are not typically known for their flexibility. However, we designed small, fixed trapezoidal pedestals, strategically placed within the room to accommodate the plumbing, electrical and technology requirements. We then configured moveable trapezoidal tables to accommodate a lecture/demonstration-type delivery whereby all of the students would be facing forward and the tables can be rearranged so that pupils can work in small groups or as a whole class.

The performing arts area, specifically the auditorium component, is the most expensive real estate in a school, and usually the most underutilized. We wanted to design a space that would be community accessible and during the school day be the most used area within the building. We created two large areas in the rear of the auditorium directly behind a sloped seating section that could either create enclosed large-group lecture instruction rooms or be additional sloped seating for a performance in the auditorium. This is accomplished by the walls, floors and seating rotating and allowing the flexibility needed. This space is used by the community, professional organizations and the school district on a continuous basis.

From the High School of the Future one can see a focus on ensuring that a clear, educational vision is in place to meet both the immediate and long-term futures for lifelong learners. An important emphasis is placed on the key concepts of continuity, relevance and adaptability. Such a focus ensures a reduction in time wasted in moving from one learning area to another and the belief that learning can take place in all areas of the school and at all times of the day. That relevance means the focus on a move from the traditional model of box-like classrooms linked by corridors to a reflection of modern life with street spaces, mall-like eating areas and inspirational use of bright, welcoming public spaces. The awareness now of a range of learning styles and the need for wide-ranging teaching strategies suggests that teaching spaces must be both larger and also more flexible. The use of easily moveable walls and flexible furnishing clearly enables rooms to be used in a range of ways, enabling kinaesthetic learning to take place. It may also be possible, in larger rooms, to create a range of different learning spaces with a soft seating or beanbag area, a large open area for movement and easily portable desks that can be arranged in different formats.

Reflection

To what extent can lighting and colour influence learning in your classroom?

How might your current buildings provide limitations to continuous learning, and how might you be able to overcome these limits?

How might you redesign the use of furniture in your room to increase learning strategies?

To what extent does your current school building reflect the current focus on energy saving and sustainability?

Have you considered how initially higher capital costs may bring about long-term energy savings?

Is your learning space large enough to enable flexible, individualized learning to take place?

How does new technology currently fit into your school buildings?

A number of interesting studies continue to take place into the influence of light, colour and space on learning development. In Alberta, Canada, researchers noted that attendance was improved through more regular exposure to daylight and natural, full-spectrum lighting. There were also other benefits from exposure to vitamin D through lighting, such as reduced dental cavities and increased growth—more than 1.9 cm in two years. A further study in North Carolina in the USA indicated that students taught in natural daylight conditions gained higher test score improvements in maths and English than those taught in the more usual non-daylight conditions. Clearly, this is an area of study that requires more large-scale research over a range of conditions and learning styles.

> *The speaker and the school master, and the third grown person*
> *present, all backed a little, and swept with their eyes the inclined*
> *plane of little vessels then and there arranged in order, ready to*
> *have imperial gallons of facts poured into them until they were full*
> *to the brim.*
>
> *Charles Dickens,* **Hard Times**

We need to move from the world of Charles Dickens to a learning experience that more closely reflects the 21st-century world.

In contrast to Dickens, Randall Fielding (2006), in his article "Learning, Lighting and Colour", writes:

> *... an effective learning environment in the 21st century has little*
> *in common with the rows of classrooms and desks or child factories*
> *of the industrial or information age.*

We have moved from the industrial revolution to the technological revolution, demanding different skills from our young people. Our students no longer need to work in artificially lit rooms focusing forward onto a brighter area, as they may have done 50 years ago. The skills of adhering to a set routine with long periods of enforced concentration for specific periods of time are now replaced by the skills of pattern recognition and the ability to extrapolate relevant ideas from a mass of information. Workers of the future need to have the analytical and logical skills of the 20th century but also those whole-mind attributes of empathy, emotional intelligence and the ability to see the big picture.

Using the new technologies

Having noted the significance of light and colour and the need for flexible spaces, it is important to refer to the use of the ever-progressing digital technology that our students are using. Previous radical attempts to change the learning process or design new learning environments have lacked the driving force of information and communication technology (ICT), which is now ubiquitous and generally reliable. We can now access managed online services and resources, which can enable learning progress to take place as never before. The pace of change already referred to points to the view that learning in 10 years' time is likely to be quite different from that today. Young people's digital lifestyles challenge the relevance of current curriculum and learning processes. In planning our learning environments we appear to face two likely futures—those of the children we now have in our care and the future of their children.

We are now able to build a learner-centric approach, harnessing the flexibility of anytime, anywhere learning through mobile technology. The development of wireless Internet and increasing use of learning platforms and e-portals enables us to make learning a far more continuous process, not governed by the school bell or the need to book a specialist room several days in advance. The power of mobile technology can also help overcome some of the environmental limitations of buildings designed for another age or purpose.

A review of Maslow and Frager's (1954) hierarchy of needs would seem to indicate the potential power of ICT to build on a sense of belonging, enhance aesthetic needs and develop self-fulfilment. Our students are no longer bounded by the walls of our classrooms or the timings of the school day. Why should our students learn French in a class with 25 other non-French-speaking students when they could converse on a daily basis with their peers in France? Why teach the theory of cash flow in business studies when our students have the opportunity to manage an online company offering real solutions to actual problems?

Reflection

How does the use of ICT enhance your students' learning?

To what extent do you harness the digital talents of your learners?

Do you teach ICT or use the skills to underpin the learning process?

To what extent is ICT literacy a key skill of the 21st century?

How do you use new technology to replicate the working world?

To what extent do you use technology to enhance international understanding?

In considering the impact of continuing development of the use of new technologies on our learning environment, it is worth keeping in mind the words of Alan November (2001):

> *The real revolution is not about technology. It's about accessing information and communication. It's not about the wires, it's about what flows through them. We need to teach students how to read the "grammar" of the Internet and apply strategies to validate the information on websites.*

The challenge of sustainability

As we seek to refocus our view of the learning environment from the angle of the 21st century, we increasingly need to do so in the context of global environmental change. Sustainability in terms of energy-saving, waste recycling and a raised awareness of our impact on our environment is an important aspect whereby our learning environment can literally be part of the learning process.

In Australia, the Sustainable Schools Initiative aims to embed the key concepts within the culture of learning. Whole-school approaches are supported to bring about educational, environmental, social and financial benefits and encourage direct student involvement in the values of sustainability.

How aware are you of your carbon footprint (a measure of how much land and water are needed to produce the resources needed and to get rid of the waste that one generates)? An awareness of our carbon footprint can help us understand why we need to use our resources more carefully and gives us a clearer view of our roles as global citizens.

In designing our learning environments we need to reflect the values of sustainability through grey-water recycling systems, solar power and energy-saving lighting. We also need to involve students in long-term recycling processes.

As with all learning processes, the concept of working with students, rather than transmitting learning to them, generates a level of ownership and involvement that enables students to make full use of their learning preferences in a flexible, sustainable, well-planned environment.

As teachers and school leaders, it would seem axiomatic that we should strive to remove physical, sensory, geographical or cultural barriers to students' participation in learning. However, it is very likely that all teachers and students will be able to provide examples of how our rooms, furniture, heating, lighting, walls and access to technology may have been amended easily and economically in order to strengthen relationships, raise motivation and increase student and teacher engagement in the effective learning process.

The IB learner profile in schools focuses on the culture and ethos of the school. There is a realization that as we develop more personalized approaches to learning, using new technologies, and brain-based and thinking skills strategies based upon personalized learning styles, we may now be inhibited by a school designed for a different world of learning.

> *The IB ... invites schools to evaluate critically their learned environment and make the changes necessary ... Such changes should lead to a truly collaborative learning environment.*

Whether the changes called for are predominantly to the physical learning environment or to the ethos, culture and atmosphere of learning, they require a clear vision of 21st-century lifelong learning skills, an openness of mind and the energy and commitment to enable our young people to develop as global citizens.

As Dryden and Vos (2001) noted, "for the first time in history anything is possible", so we must ensure that we meet the challenge of the learning environment by innovation and creativity founded on the received views of all parts of our school community. Whether, as in the High School of the Future, we have the opportunity to build a flexible, learning environment founded on the latest technology or, as in the case of the Franklyn Science Academy in Philadelphia, we open in a refurbished office block, we can develop our environment to meet the lifelong learning needs of our students. Our environment can inspire and enhance learning but it cannot replace the essential human relationships that truly underpin effective learning.

CHAPTER 7

Assessment for learning

In 2006 the IB published an IB learner profile booklet, which set out what IB learners at all stages should strive to be.

The very first quality identified in the IB learner profile is for learners to be inquirers:

> They develop their natural curiosity. They acquire the skills necessary to conduct inquiry and research and show independence in learning. They actively enjoy learning and this love of learning will be sustained throughout their lives.

Who could possibly disagree with such a principle? And, yet, how should this be achieved, how should we inculcate such skills in the minds of young people; in short, how do we create independent learners? How can we explore the challenge of developing independent learners in terms of assessment?

The IB certainly recognizes some of the issues confronting teachers and asks:

> In formative assessment tasks, do we provide students with enough opportunities to take intellectual risks, and then support them in taking such risks?

> To what extent does the range of assessment strategies we use meet the diverse needs of students and encourage creative and critical thinking?

> Can we provide time for students to reflect on an assessment task and what they have learnt from it?

> What aspects of students' development do we report on?
> (IB Learner Profile Booklet)

Paul Black and Dylan Wiliam (1998) make a telling point when they observe that:

> While students' learning can be advanced by feedback through comments, the giving of marks does not usually help and, moreover, has a negative effect in that students ignore comments when marks are also given.

This certainly echoes our experience as students ourselves—the higher the mark out of 10, 20 or 100, the better we were and, correspondingly, the lower the mark, the worse we were. Only as one advances beyond the ages of 16 and 18 do comments begin to assume the significance that is at the heart of formative assessment; do they actually help create the independent learner, one who is able to reflect on his or her learning in a way that enhances it.

Over the past few years a key psychological factor has emerged in influencing levels of maturity and disaffection in almost all levels of society and, indeed, disaffection in schools: the "locus of control". This concept is closely linked to others, such as self-esteem and self-efficacy, and it is rapidly becoming a key factor in developing students' motivation and engagement. Students are, after all, active rather than passive participants in the learning process.

In a sense, all this begs two questions—to what extent has formative assessment or, as it is now more commonly known, "assessment for learning" been the poor relation to assessment of learning, and how far have teachers been able to develop the skills needed to use assessment for learning effectively? There is little doubt that across many countries standardized testing has come to rule the roost, and this has usually been associated with a prescribed curriculum that almost always sets great store on the twin pillars of literacy and numeracy. This is particularly evident in both the UK and the USA and has often resulted in a punishment–reward strategy and a narrowing of the curriculum in order to provide more time for literacy and numeracy activities. In "The condition of public education: the 14th Bracy Report", Bracy (2004) notes that typical headlines for many US schools proclaim:

> *To give their third graders an extra 50 minutes of reading daily, the principal has eliminated music, art and gym.*

and

> *Raymond Middle School lost its two art teachers last year. Home economics was eliminated along with most foreign language classes and some physical education classes.*

In the UK there has been a sharp drop in the number of students taking a foreign language since it became an optional subject between the ages of 14 and 16, and there is actually evidence to suggest that there has been a narrowing of the curriculum in the UK to ensure that an increasing number of students reach the magical five A*–C level at the General Certificate of Secondary Education (GCSE).

On a brighter note, however, it is clear that the British government has become alarmed by this trend and is taking steps to rectify the problem by renovating its curriculum provision for those between the ages of 11 and 16.

Notwithstanding this, it is unclear how far approaches to assessment for learning have permeated the thinking of teachers in all schools (whether state, private or international). As Fullan, Hill and Crevola (2006) would have it, "Schools need to get assessment for learning out of the basement, clean it up, and creatively recombine it with personalization and continuous professional learning". They go on to quote D R Sadler (1989), who set out the challenge for assessment for learning in 1982 by suggesting that teachers focus on "how judgements about the quality of student response (performances, pieces or works) can be used to shape and improve the student's competence by short-circuiting the randomness and inefficiency of trial and error learning". He further suggested that the essential element of formative assessment was "feedback", which would allow the student opportunities to perceive the standard he or she was aiming for against a current level of performance. Feedback would then help the student close that gap.

Key questions

To what extent is your teaching style interactive?

Are students able to work together to find an answer to a problem?

Is your school's marking policy supportive of formative assessment by concentrating on comments and targets rather than targets and grades?

How do you ask questions in class?

Is there an opportunity for peer marking in the lesson?

Are decision-making processes with regard to students fair?

Do you pay the right amount of attention to differentiation when giving feedback to students?

Do you use active revision strategies with your students?

Are you able to analyse student performance data and results and make critical use of them?

Do you work with other teachers in developing assessment for learning strategies?

Are you able to observe other teachers and give feedback, and are you regularly observed yourself?

Taken together, these questions represent a very significant challenge to all schools, even accepting the fact that some schools are further down the line than others. The challenge comes in various forms:

- ▶ change management
- ▶ continuous professional development
- ▶ teamwork
- ▶ school culture.

CASE STUDY

St Cecilia's Catholic Infant and Nursery School/Liverpool, UK

Assessment for Learning

Over four years ago, St Cecilia's infants became involved in a number of projects that have focused on continued development of children's involvement in their own learning. While recognizing the value of summative assessments to record achievement, as a school we were particularly keen to make formative assessment more meaningful for both the teacher and the child.

In 2005 we participated in the Assessment for Learning project, which focused on utilizing and developing a range of strategies that placed the child clearly at the centre of the assessment process. One of the chief principles of Assessment for Learning is that promoting the involvement of pupils in assessment allows them to take ownership of their learning. Through the sharing of learning intentions and goals and the establishment of success criteria, the learner becomes more actively involved. The teacher plays a significant role in modelling for the children the learning strategies, attributes, skills and standards.

One strategy that has proved to be particularly successful across the whole school is the use of "What Makes Good?". This flexible approach can be used in wide-ranging contexts, from behaviours (e.g. "What makes a good line/listener/friend?" to the more academic (e.g. "What makes a good story/reader/writer?"). The use of "Golden Sentences" supports young children in their emerging understanding of sentence construction and it can be adapted to accommodate sentences of increasing complexity. "Three stars and a wish" is a strategy that the teacher can use to identify three positive aspects of the child's work and it also provides a challenging but achievable target for the child. Spider diagrams are used frequently in order to establish children's initial understanding of a concept. Having kept this, they can later be added to in order to demonstrate the learning that has taken place. For our older children, as part of the assessment continuum, we have integrated peer and self-assessment strategies, which allow children the opportunity to take increasing responsibility in moving their learning forward.

In St Cecilia's, Assessment for Learning has had a significant impact in making target-setting more meaningful and personalized for both children and teachers.

To give a flavour of the challenge confronting us, think about the concept of "wait time", that is the period of silence that teachers allow after asking a question before, if no answer is forthcoming, asking another question or answering their own question. "Astoundingly it often amounted to less than a second" (Rowe 1986). And, of course, it follows that the only way this could work was for the answer to be based on a memorized fact. A challenge, then, is for the teacher, and also the department, to change. If this is raised to the level of the school, then the challenge is even greater. Integration is probably a key issue in many secondary schools, because of the high commitment of most teachers towards their subject disciplines. Somehow departments and staff have to enhance one another's contribution to the achievement of the main purpose of the school. Getting teachers to become "assessment literate", in the words of Hargreaves and Fullan, requires an extremely high degree of collaborative working and much reflection on current pedagogical practice.

Eliciting students' values on some of these issues is essential because for some schools it provides a starting point and for others an indication of just how far down the road they have travelled. Schools need to know how far their students have become participants and not victims in the assessment process and how far the "locus of control" has shifted their way. This is not to say, however, that shifting the locus of control necessarily entails a loss of control by the teacher; rather, it is about the sharing of responsibility. Black and Wiliam (1998) identified three crucial elements in developing assessment for learning strategies.

Questioning

The research on "wait time" has already been referred to. The shorter the wait time, the greater the reliance on factual questions. For those involved in developing new assessment strategies, this approach has been superseded by concentrating on questions that will stimulate whole-class discussion or in many cases asking students to look at a number of questions which they might use to explore a particular topic. The advantage to this approach is that it allows teachers an opportunity to explore the degree of understanding exhibited by their students on particular topics.

Learning to learn is a fundamental element of this approach, particularly for those students who are experiencing difficulties. The competitive element in "spotting the right answer" gives way to developing levels of understanding.

Marking and comments

This chapter began by observing that grades and marks undermine whatever comments are posted on students' work. It does not follow, though, that all comments are helpful. As Black and Wiliam (1998) observe:

> ... *comments become useful feedback only if students use them to guide further work.*

It follows that teachers need to become more adept in their use of comments and more sophisticated in the ways in which they follow up such comments.

> How far have you/the department/the school moved from marking through comments and grades to comments and targets only?
>
> How are you able to determine if students have addressed your comments?
>
> How are you able to accommodate the learning needs of individual students?
>
> How much attention do you pay to differentiation in your feedback to students?
>
> Have your students changed in the way in which they view the role of their written work?

Self-assessment and peer assessment

The research on this aspect of assessment for learning points to three significant advantages for both the teacher and the learner:

- The language used is that of the student.
- The student is given an opportunity to play the role of the teacher.
- There appears to be a greater willingness to pursue the quest for an explanation of the topic with other students than is often the case with the teacher. There is a variety of reasons for this, but one which stands out is that the student feels less intimidated with his or her peers than with the teacher.

There is a growing body of evidence that delineates assessment as a key element in the workings of "effective" departments in schools. In one such study by Alma Harris, Ian Jamieson and Jen Russ (1997), it is observed that:

> ... *efforts were made to try and give the students, particularly the older ones, a stake in the assessment. They were often invited to mark each other's and their own work and discuss their marks with the teacher in order to try and understand the strengths and weaknesses of their own efforts ... the assessment system was used as the vehicle for frequent feedback to the students, feedback that tended to be more criterion that norm referenced and these assessment-linked activities tended to provide the students with a clear sense of progression, which assisted motivation. In particular, it allowed them to highlight some of their own weaknesses on which they could concentrate.*

There is a very clear correlation between student engagement with school and student empowerment. The extent to which students play a part in the life of the school, participate in the planning process and are listened to significantly affects their identification with the school and with their education.

Formative assessment

Formative assessment strategies go a long way to reinforcing this sense of identification. Consulting students' attitudes and sampling their opinion is a powerful way to kick-start a process or to determine how successful the department/school has been in delivering new strategies.

Strategy

Devise a student questionnaire to test student opinion in the following areas:
- identification with school
- self-esteem
- behaviour
- teacher support for student learning.

Implicit in such an activity will be questions designed to flesh out opinions on teacher fairness, how interesting work is, whether teachers help students understand their work, how they can help make work better, the extent to which the school encourages independent thinking (an important element of the IB learner profile) and how far students have confidence in themselves and confidence that teachers listen to what they say. In phrasing the questions, account must obviously be taken of the differences between the ages of the children being sampled and the nature of the school. Harris, Jameson and Russ's study of effective departments serves to reinforce the importance of engaging meaningfully with students:

> We found that there were several aspects of whole-school policy that our departments were actually building upon. The first was a stress on the importance of the students that clearly went beyond the usual professional rhetoric. The schools in our study were characterised by systematic developments aimed at providing a caring environment for students, and every effort was made to involve them fully in the life of the school.

At an individual classroom level this was translated into:

- ▶ an involvement of students in the learning process
- ▶ cooperative learning among students
- ▶ engaging students in reviewing the learning process
- ▶ ensuring that the assessment process was fundamental to building motivation and confidence
- ▶ using data as a tool for empowering teaching and learning.

The learning organization

Of course, this is about more than just assessment—this is really the core of good teaching and, of course, there are implications for pedagogy, professional learning, theories of learning, and leadership and management. This is best illustrated by Figure 7.1.

Figure 7.1: Venn diagram (Fullan 2001; adapted from Louis and Kruse 1995, Newman and Wehlage 1995)

In this model, teachers become "assessment literate". They engage in collaborative activity to create a professional learning community, which in turn informs classroom pedagogy. Most recently, Fullan, Hill and Crevola (2006) have modified "professional learning community" into "professional learning", believing that every teacher needs to engage in daily ongoing learning.

Assessment for learning is not a "bolt-on" technique; it requires a sea change in the way in which teachers operate in the classroom so that:

▶ The focus of control becomes a shared activity between the teacher and the learner.

▶ The student becomes an active learner.

▶ The student becomes an independent learner.

▶ Greater emphasis is placed on what Black and Wiliam call "pedagogical content knowledge". This is less about subject knowledge and more about "the teacher's capacity to explore and interpret the subject matter [to develop] effective pedagogy". Some commentators have called this "focused teaching" (Fullan, Hall and Crevola 2006), in which specific teaching strategies and methods are linked to learning objectives, standards and targets.

A skills approach to the curriculum

The IB, in developing its Primary and Middle Years Programmes, recognized that it is not always helpful, from a learner's point of view, to compartmentalize subjects. Correspondingly, making connections between subjects through the use of themes and key skills or competencies provides greater insights into the subject matter being taught. In particular, one of the IB's publications, *Today's Students for Tomorrow's World,* describes the programmes approaches to teaching and learning.

> *The programmes teach students to think critically, and encourage them to draw connections between areas of knowledge and to use problem solving techniques and concepts from many disciplines.*

> *They teach students how to learn including how to analyse information; how to develop, organise and present their ideas; how to access information from the library, the Internet and other media; how to work independently and collaborate with others; and how to solve problems.*

Taking this a stage further, the Middle Year Programme's *A Basis for Practice* booklet suggests that this is a curriculum which:

> *calls for more than "knowing": it involves reflective thinking,*
> *both critical and creative, about ideas and behaviours. It includes*
> *problem-solving and analysis, clarification and discussion of*
> *personal beliefs and standards on which decisions are made. It also*
> *leads to critical thinking and action.*

This approach is increasingly being adopted through a range of learning models for students aged 11 years and upwards, most notably the "Opening Minds" framework developed by the Royal Society of Arts in the UK.

Increasingly, knowledge has a provisional status and the Internet is providing a hugely increasing and ever-changing body of knowledge, which highlights the need to promote skills in finding, analysing and evaluating information so that learners can construct their own knowledge. Moreover, Charles Handy (1998), has pointed out the need to develop interpersonal and social skills, to become emotionally intelligent, in order to cope with changes to the workplace and the emergence of "portfolio" people.

The leadership dimension

It must be said that little of this will come to fruition unless there is a clear understanding of the role of leadership and management. There is a multitude of books and articles on this topic, but if any of the above are to be implemented then most of the following observations will need to be present in the model that underpins the leadership of the school:

- ▶ understanding change and, by definition, leading and managing it
- ▶ building relationships and motivating and managing people
- ▶ knowledge creation and sharing
- ▶ coherence-making through designing and aligning systems
- ▶ capacity building in the organization.

Much of this chapter has focused on the implications for students and teachers of new assessment strategies and how they will transform classroom practice and indeed transform the role of students in the school. Indeed, by concentrating on the student, most of the above dimensions will be, of necessity, activated. Certainly, Senge (2000) holds this as a truism:

> *I have come to believe that the real hope for deep and enduring*
> *processes of evolution in school lies with students. They have a*
> *deep passion for making schools work. They are connected to the*
> *future in the ways no adult is.*

This is echoed by Papert (1996), who suggests that child power is the most powerful change force of all, and by Hartle and Hobby (2003), who argue that:

> *The growing importance of knowledge puts a new premium on learning and suggests a revaluation of the respective roles of teacher and learner. The changes ... challenge our received views of the curriculum, assessment and the role of teachers.*

They have reflected their thinking in Figure 7.2.

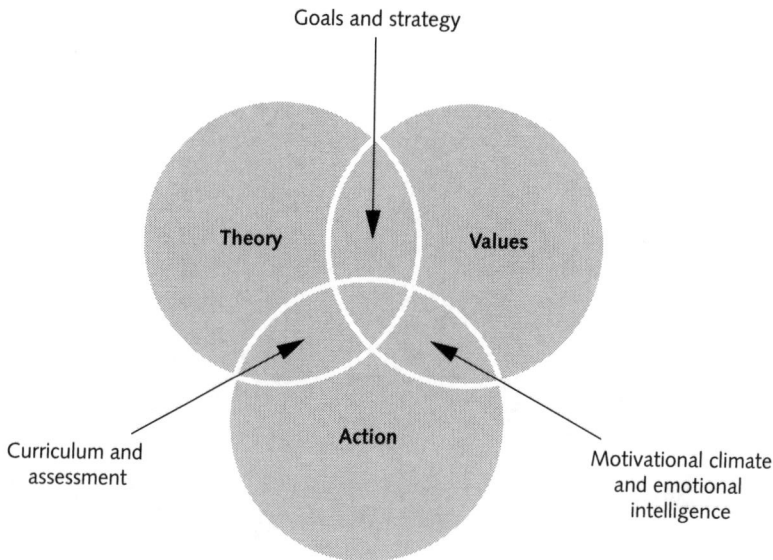

Figure 7.2: Hartle and Hobby's Venn diagram

The most fitting comment about the development of schools as learning communities and how assessment for learning is changing the role of teachers and learners comes from Senge (2000), who suggests that a learning school is:

> *Not so much ... a separate place (for it may not stay in one place) as a meeting ground for learning ... dedicated to the idea that all those involved with it will be continually enhancing and expanding their awareness and capabilities. A learning school puts the students at the centre and connects up students, teachers, leaders, schools and communities.*

CHAPTER 8

Leading the learning organization

If there is an all-pervasive theme to this book it must be the challenge of change, and not just change but "exponential change". How this is managed is crucial to the success of all educational institutions. In *The Learning Organisation*, Garrett (1987) argues that, for an organization to survive and develop, the rate of learning within it must be equal to, or greater than, the rate of change in the external environment. To achieve this it is therefore necessary for a school to become a learning organization. This argument is reinforced by Peters and Waterman (1995), who assert that such organizations have developed a set of strategies that encourage experiments in change and embrace a commitment to all things new.

Charles Handy (1991) provides two definitions of a learning organization: an organization that learns and an organization that encourages learning in its people. Michael Fullan is a passionate champion of the concept of professional learning committees, which enables teachers to learn from each other and schools to learn from each other. Most recently, in the *McKinsey Quarterly* (2007), Bryan and Joyce suggest that:

> For the better part of two decades, companies have invested heavily in knowledge management—with limited results because real value comes less from managing knowledge than from creating and exchanging it. To promote the exchange of knowledge, companies must remove the structural barriers to the interactions of professionals and managers as they solve problems.

The key message these days is to make organizations work better. For the world of education, and in particular, schools, this is a challenge.

Almost any author you care to select who is writing on the subject of school management and leadership will constantly refer to the "challenge" facing school leaders, the need to understand and manage "change", and the complex problems facing education and schools. Brent Davies and Linda Ellison (1997), in their book *School Leadership in the 21st Century*, suggest that:

> *Faced with the increasing complexities of the modern world, school*
> *leaders need to understand three key perspectives, each of which*
> *is itself operating at three different levels, namely that of the*
> *wider global environment, that of the organisation and that of the*
> *individual.*

Dean Fink (2005) is also trenchant in his views regarding the issue of school leadership:

> *[It] is my conviction that the contemporary state of education*
> *internationally, and of educational leadership in particular, limits*
> *student learning, stultifies teacher creativity and professionalism,*
> *and discourages people that have the ability and passion to lead*
> *our schools and educate our children for the emerging knowledge*
> *society.*

Hargreaves (2005) reinforces this point in a chapter he contributed to *The Essentials of School Leadership*. He believes that there is a crisis of leadership throughout society from which education is not exempted: "in education, leadership is also in crisis. Not only is leadership losing its lustre, it is also losing its people". He goes on to suggest that, as the "Boomer" generation of leaders retire, it is becoming increasingly difficult to recruit new leaders to public services as a result of the stresses of change and the fact that "leadership itself is also changing". This is not to say that there is any lack of advice about how to chart a pathway through these difficulties; indeed, the topic of leadership has become a growth industry, with scores of books on organizational theory, change management, leadership styles and strategic planning, so much so that schools are almost overwhelmed by them. The picture is further complicated by the assertions of writers such as Belinda Harris (2007), who suggests that:

> *Rational models of leadership simply "cannot hold" in the*
> *21st century school. Educational change places high demand*
> *for personal change. New ways of leading are needed that*
> *acknowledge leadership as primarily an emotional and not a*
> *rational activity.*

Perhaps by recognizing some basic principles we might at least begin to probe some possible approaches to the whole issue of leading a learning organization. The first is to reiterate a point that Stoll, Fink and Earl (2003) make—that "leadership for learning is not a destination ... but a journey with plenty of detours ... Effective educational leaders are continuously open to new learnings because the journey keeps changing".

Perhaps more important is an observation that Fink (2005) made in a recent publication, *Leadership for Mortals*:

> Leadership in a school does not rest exclusively on the shoulders of a few formal leaders. Leadership is everywhere. It is like culture; it is intangible, non-rational (echoing Harris's point) and non-linear. You see it only in its results. Every person in the school exercises some form of influence over others and directs in some way the daily course of events.

Pick up almost any book on educational management or strategic leadership and inevitably most of the content will relate in some way to how the structure of the school affects human resource management (including appraisal/performance management and equal opportunities), managing the curriculum, managing learning and teaching, managing finance, managing health and safety, managing teams and a host of other educational functions in the school. Of course, they all need to be managed and of course they are all fundamental to a successful school, but, as many writers now accept, the culture within which these take place is fundamental to a school's continued and successful development. Moreover, if it is true that a concern about structure is increasingly subordinate to a concern about culture, then it is probably true to say that the concept of building learning organizations and communities is now taking precedence over "going it alone" and that an emphasis on emotional leadership is gaining ground over a concentration on leadership styles and other managerial activities described above.

School culture

Louise Stoll (1999) maintains that "school culture is one of the most complex and important concepts in education—it has also been one of the most neglected". In 1994 Hargreaves was already warning that:

> Schools and teachers are being affected more and more by the demands and contingencies of an increasingly complex and fast-paced postmodern world. Yet their response is often inappropriate or ineffective—leaving intact the systems and structures of the present, or retreating to comforting myths of the past.

The question is, then: "Are there different types of school culture?" For example, Rosenholtz (1989), suggested that there were "moving" and "stuck" schools. This contrasting model was refined by Hopkins into four expressions of school culture (Figure 8.1).

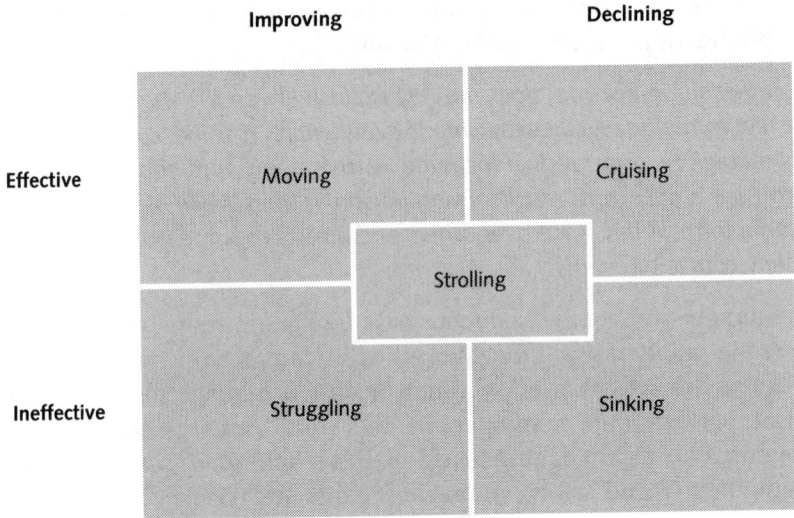

Figure 8.1: Hopkins' school culture model

Stoll and Fink (1995) elaborated a series of positive cultural norms that can be applied to schools:

1   Shared goals: "we know where we're going".
2   Responsibility for success: "we must succeed".
3   Collegiality: "we're working on this together".
4   Continuous improvement: "we can get better".
5   Lifelong learning: "learning is for everyone".
6   Risk-taking: "we learn by trying something new".
7   Support: "there's always someone there to help".
8   Mutual respect: "everyone has something to offer".
9   Openness: "we can discuss our differences".
10   Celebration and humour: "we feel good about ourselves"

Dean Fink has taken the Hopkins model and positive cultural norms, which he articulated with Louise Stoll, and linked them to two questionnaires (one from the Halton Board of Education in 1988), which allow schools to determine how effective they are and whether school improvement is being promoted or hindered.

- Complete the School Effectiveness and the Cultural Norms inventories.
- Add up the number of items in each inventory that you ticked as 4s and 5s.
- Apply the totals to the School Typology chart, with School Effectiveness on the vertical axis and Cultural Norms on the horizontal.

How effective is your school?		Never	Rarely	Sometimes	Often	Always
1	Instructional leadership (firm and purposeful, a participative approach, the leading professional)	1	2	3	4	5
2	Shared vision and clear goals (unity of purpose, consistency of practice)	1	2	3	4	5
3	Shared values and beliefs	1	2	3	4	5
4	A learning environment (an orderly atmosphere, an attractive working environment)	1	2	3	4	5
5	Teaching and curriculum focus (maximization of learning time, academic emphasis, focus on achievement)	1	2	3	4	5
6	High expectations (for all, communication of expectations, intellectual challenge for all)	1	2	3	4	5

How effective is your school?		Never	Rarely	Sometimes	Often	Always
7	Positive student behaviour (clear and fair discipline and feedback)	1	2	3	4	5
8	Frequent monitoring of student progress (ongoing monitoring, evaluating school performance)	1	2	3	4	5
9	Student involvement and responsibility (high student self-esteem, positions of responsibility, control of work)	1	2	3	4	5
10	Climate for learning (positive physical environment, recognition, incentives)	1	2	3	4	5
11	Teacher collegiality and development (school-based staff development)	1	2	3	4	5
12	Parental and community involvement and support	1	2	3	4	5

Do the cultural norms of your school promote school improvement?		Never	Rarely	Sometimes	Often	Always
1	Shared goals (we know where we're going)	1	2	3	4	5
2	Responsibility for success (we must succeed)	1	2	3	4	5
3	Collegiality (we're working on it together)	1	2	3	4	5
4	Continuous improvement (we can get better)	1	2	3	4	5
5	Lifelong learning (learning is for everyone)	1	2	3	4	5
6	Risk taking (we learn by trying something new)	1	2	3	4	5
7	Support (there's always someone here to help)	1	2	3	4	5
8	Mutual support (everyone has something to offer)	1	2	3	4	5
9	Openness (we can discuss our differences)	1	2	3	4	5
10	Celebration and humour (we feel good about ourselves)	1	2	3	4	5

Rosenholtz's 1989 publication *Teachers Workplace: The Social Organisation of Schools* developed a typology of school culture predicated on the model of a "moving" and a "stuck" school (Figure 8.2). This has been further elaborated by Stoll and Fink (1995), who attempt to indicate the level of dynamism in a school on the basis of two dimensions: "effectivenes—ineffectiveness" and "improving—declining". Moving schools keep developing and are deemed to be effective in value-added terms; cruising schools appear to be effective but in reality are just "marking time"; strolling schools are neither one nor the other but are not responding quickly enough to the demands of change and struggling schools are, as the title suggests, ineffective and incapable of coping with change.

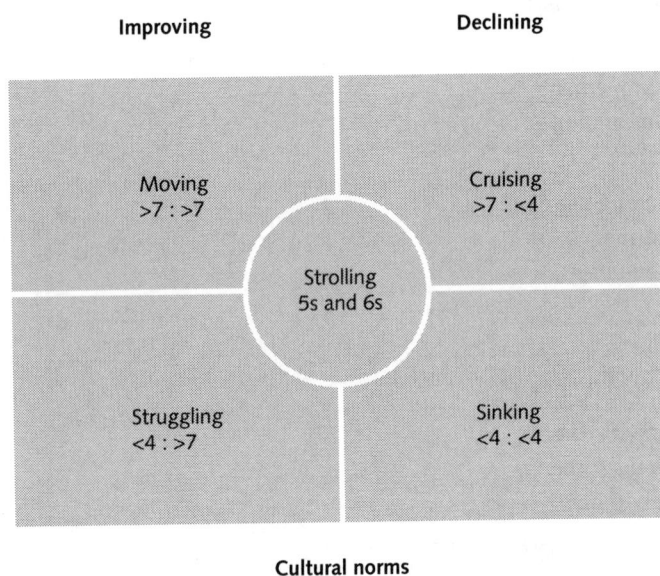

Figure 8.2: Stoll and Fink school typology

Deal and Kennedy (1983) offer some further practical guidance for schools interested in examining their individualism:

1 Get to know your culture—ask teachers, students, parents, non-teaching staff and other involved participants what the school really stands for; note how people spend their time; find out who are the heroines, spies and other roles in the cultural network, and reflect on the values they represent.

2 Consider how the school culture encourages or inhibits student progress, development and achievement, and the accomplishment of school goals. Examine people's values to see whether they are the same or whether there is a mismatch between groups.

3 Arrange opportunities where people can discuss and re-examine their values.

Before schools can embark on the path to becoming a learning organization they must create a culture that promotes not only collegiality but also the other cultural norms identified by Stoll and Fink (1995).

Becoming a learning organization

If it is true that schools are improving or declining then the central message conveyed in Handy's (1998) definition is that for a school to be effective it must become a learning organization.

In their 1992 polemic, *What's Worth Fighting for in Your School?*, Michael Fullan and Andy Hargreaves argued that:

> *We must experiment and discover better ways of working together that mobilise the power of the group while at the same time enhancing individual development. We must use collegiality not to level people down but to bring together strength and creativity.*

They asserted that schools had not yet adopted the principles of collaboration, collegiality, joint and mutual observations of lessons and "interactive professionalism". While it is clear that this situation has significantly improved, it has not yet reached the stage described by Rosenholtz where "it is assumed that improvement in teaching is a collective rather than an individual enterprise, and that analysis, evaluation, and experimentation in concert with colleagues are conditions under which teachers improve".

Stoll and Fink (1995) suggest eight criteria that help define a learning organization:

1 Treat teachers as professionals—they require knowledge about child development, emotional intelligence, assessment for learning, teaching and learning styles and a host of other emergent themes in education. "Teachers need to become knowledgeable about policy and about professional and research issues."
2 Promote high-quality staff development.
3 Encourage teacher leadership and participation. As Fullan and Hargreaves observe, "every teacher is a leader. Depending on life and career circumstances, the leadership role at some stages will be significant."
4 Promote collaboration for improvement.

5 Develop ways to induct, include and develop new members of the organization.

6 Function successfully within their context—learning organizations exist within the context of a nation, a community and, often, a district. They constantly read their various contexts and develop the political skills to function successfully within these contexts.

7 Work to change things that matter.

8 "Sweat the small stuff"—learning organizations have processes and procedures in place, which staff, students and parents trust. Effective administration of day-to-day activities, what some may consider the "small stuff", is fundamental to the development of a learning organization.

In *Sustainable Leadership* Andy Hargreaves and Dean Fink (2006) explicitly refer to the role of the head teacher in creating a learning organization:

> *One of the keys to achieving the cohesion and dynamism of a strong professional learning community is in how leadership is stretched over the school.*

and

> *In the context of professional learning communities, strong leaders are not strident and forceful. Although their commitment to all students' learning needs to be insistently and clearly voiced, their true strengths may be in:*
> ▶ *Modelling and building strong and rewarding relationships by paying attention to the human side of school change*
> ▶ *Establishing a high-trust environment*
> ▶ *Developing and renewing a culture of learning and improvement at all levels through problem solving, inquiry, and intelligent, evidence-informed decision making*
> ▶ *Helping the school community develop and commit to a cohesive and compelling purpose that also prevents dissipation of initiative and effort*
> ▶ *Stimulating a culture of professional entrepreneurship in regard to innovations and ideas that benefit student learning*
> ▶ *Establishing and enforcing grown-up professional norms of civil argument and productive debate*
> ▶ *Ensuring that the voices of minority members of the culture always receive a proper hearing*
> ▶ *Doing all this within an unswerving commitment to improving learning and achievement for all students, especially those who are further behind.*

How this applies to your school might be examined further through this self-reflective exercise.

Reflection

As a school leader, ask yourself whether you can give an affirmative answer to the following questions:

Do you provide enough time for teachers to reflect individually on their values and ideas?

Do you encourage teachers to obtain high-quality feedback from students, parents and colleagues on their work?

Are you developing a risk-taking culture in the school?

How far is there distributed leadership in the school, which encourages shared decision-making and problem-solving?

Is there a commitment to collaborative working in the school?

Do you actively encourage teachers to understand the culture of the school?

Do you encourage a work–life balance in the school?

Is there a commitment to continuous improvement and lifelong learning?

Do you monitor the connection between teacher development and student attainment and learning?

Emotional leadership

Elsewhere in this book, it has been argued that the emergence of "emotional leadership" is now of prime importance for schools. Harris (2007) holds that:

> Leadership is essentially about leadership practices not leadership tasks. Developing understanding of interpersonal processes is fundamental if leaders are to foster emotional awareness and literacy in others and engage community members in the co-creative process of learning and school improvement.

Moreover, the nature of how we learn is central to how learning organizations develop and how they are led. To quote Stoll and Fink again:

> Teacher learning has to be a goal and intermediate outcome of school improvement. In effective schools, lifelong learning incorporating adults as well as children is a norm, and emphasis is placed on developing the school as a learning organisation.

It is now widely accepted that adult learners are more self-directed, and reference has already been made to Boyatzis's *Theory of Self-Directed Learning*. A good starting point for actioning this theory is the Kolb Learning Style Inventory (LSI), which is designed to "help you understand how you learn but in educational settings and everyday life". The LSI links an individual learning style to providing greater insights for the following:

▶ how to solve problems
▶ how to work in teams
▶ how to manage disagreement and conflict
▶ how to maximize your learning from educational programmes
▶ how to make career choices
▶ how to improve personal and professional relationships.

Kolb (2005) works on the basis of a questionnaire comprising 12 questions, which are scored to show a style which is most like you to one which is least like you. The scores are then translated to a learning cycle diagram and a learning style grid, which determines your preferred learning style, of which there are four:

Learning by experiencing
▶ learning from specific experiences
▶ relating to people
▶ being sensitive to feelings and people

Learning by reflecting
▶ observing carefully before making judgments
▶ viewing issues from different perspectives
▶ looking for the meaning of things

Learning by thinking
▶ analysing ideas logically
▶ planning systematically
▶ acting on an intellectual understanding of a situation

Learning by doing
▶ showing the ability to get things done
▶ taking risks
▶ influencing people and events through action

Each learning style is associated with some basic strengths and there are suggestions for strengthening and developing each of the four styles. The LSI is an excellent tool for use in schools, particularly in the context of creating and working in teams.

Fullan (2005) uses this "Ratings" exercise to prompt leaders into reflecting about their skills in respect of emotional intelligence and to think about how they can build on their strengths and improve their weaknesses.

Identify three to five items on which you are relatively low (3 or less). How could you improve on these dimensions?

Identify three to five items on which you are relatively high (4 or 5). How could you sustain your strengths on these dimensions?

	Low				High
Self-awareness					
Emotional (reading one's own emotions and recognizing their impact: using "gut sense" to guide decisions)	1	2	3	4	5
Accurate self-assessment: (knowing one's strengths and limits)	1	2	3	4	5
Self-confidence (a sound sense of one's self-worth and capabilities)	1	2	3	4	5
Self-management					
Emotional self-control (keeping in check disruptive emotions and impulses)	1	2	3	4	5
Transparency (displaying honesty and integrity; trustworthiness)	1	2	3	4	5
Adaptability (flexibility in adapting to changing situations or overcoming obstacles)	1	2	3	4	5
Achievement (the drive to improve performance to meet internal standards of excellence)	1	2	3	4	5
Initiative (readiness to act and seize opportunities)	1	2	3	4	5

	Low				High
Optimism (seeing the up-side in events)	1	2	3	4	5
Social awareness					
Empathy (sensing others' emotions, understanding their perspective and taking active interest in their concerns)	1	2	3	4	5
Organizational awareness (reading the currents, decision networks, and politics at the organizational level)	1	2	3	4	5
Services (recognizing and meeting client or customer needs)	1	2	3	4	5
Relationship management					
Inspirational leadership (guiding and motivating with a compelling vision)	1	2	3	4	5
Influence (wielding a range of tactics for persuasion)	1	2	3	4	5
Developing others (bolstering others' abilities through feedback and guidance)	1	2	3	4	5
Change catalyst (initiating, managing and leading in a new direction)	1	2	3	4	5
Conflict management (resolving disagreements)	1	2	3	4	5
Building bonds (cultivating and maintaining a web of relationships)	1	2	3	4	5
Teamwork and collaboration (cooperation and team building)	1	2	3	4	5

Goleman, Boyatzis and McKee (2002) maintain that "groups begin to change only when they first have fully grasped the reality of how they function".

Echoing the view of Dufour and Eaker (1987), that "strong principles are crucial to the creation of learning communities", Goleman, Boyatzis and McKee (2007) suggest that creating organizations that are emotionally intelligent is also the responsibility of the "leader". This is reinforced by identifying the leadership competences that are required to develop emotionally intelligent organizations. These are:

▶ self-awareness
▶ self-management
▶ social awareness
▶ relationship management.

Hargreaves and Fink (2006) propose that "teaching and educational leadership also involve the extensive emotional labour of being responsible for motivating others and managing their moods and feelings".

In moving schools to become learning organizations, school culture and emotional leadership are the twin pillars supporting this process. By creating positive and supportive working conditions, leaders create energy, optimism and sustainability. This also sustains the change process by creating a collaborative culture, which eschews models of top-down implementation.

Moral leadership

Over the past decade much has been written about the moral dimension of leadership. This dimension or purpose is reflected by the values of leaders in the school and by the teaching staff collectively. Being aware of these values and how they can change and be applied at a particular time is a quality leaders ignore at their peril. In *Gestalt Therapy Integrated* Polster and Polster (1974) highlight how important this is:

> *Awareness is a continuous means for keeping up to date with one's self ... With each succeeding awareness one moves closer to articulating the themes of one's own life and closer also to moving towards the expression of these themes.*

Strategy

Although this can be done on an individual basis, it is also a particularly instructive group exercise.

▶ What made you go into education?
▶ What do you consider to be the major issues facing education today?
▶ What would you like your legacy, as an educator, to be?

Find out how many of the group chose which of the three questions. Ask if it was an easy or difficult choice. Select someone from each group to articulate their response and see how the discussion develops. You should find opportunities to probe some of the emotions contained in the responses, for example hope, disappointment, achievement, optimism, and so on.

These days schools need to make more use of mental models (for example, from Senge's (2000) book, *Schools that Learn*). We need to understand how we are influenced by self-generating beliefs so that our ability to achieve the results we really desire is eroded by our feelings that:

▶ our beliefs are the truth
▶ the truth is obvious
▶ our beliefs are based on real data
▶ the data we select is accurate.

Developing an awareness of emotional responses of the nature described by the ladder of inference is an important step in creating moral leadership; for example, how to deal with the moral dilemma of whether or not to hurt another person's feelings at the expense of the truth. As Harris (2007) points out, "In reality, there are no moral truths but plenty of preferences and values that guide decision making". She also fully emphasizes that school must "support robust relationships between colleagues, governors and parents that enable these difficult and sensitive ethical considerations to take place." Susan Scott (2004) has called these "fierce conversations" and they almost invariably include:

▶ presenting the issue or problem in a concise way
▶ naming the issue or problem accurately
▶ not presenting solutions too quickly
▶ discussing the "undiscussables"
▶ rethinking the term "confront" to ensure that it is not always associated with conflict
▶ recognizing that we all own a piece of the truth.

Strategy

Using the ladder of inference (Figure 8.3).

You can improve your communications by using the ladder in three ways:

▶ Becoming more aware of your own thinking and reasoning (reflection).

▶ Making your thinking and reasoning more visible to others (advocacy).

▶ Inquiring into others' thinking and reasoning (inquiry).

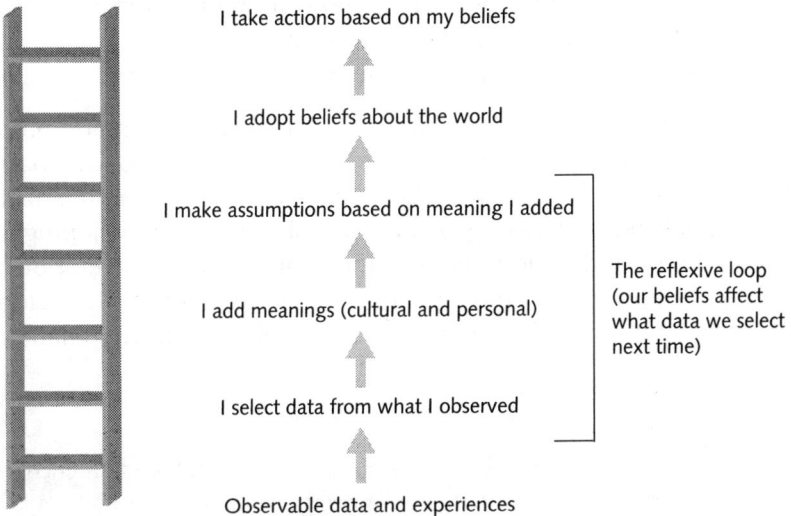

Climbing the ladder

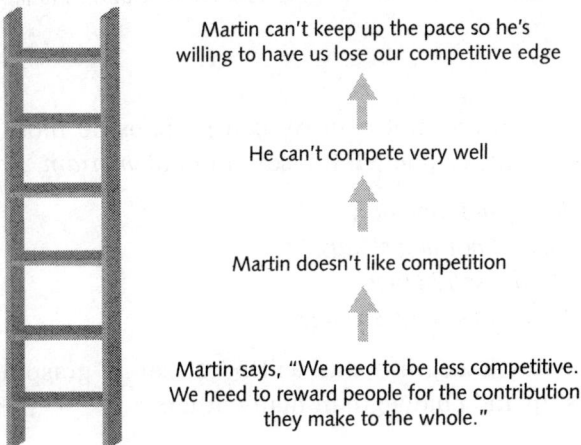

Figure 8.3: Ladder of inference

The real purpose of a "fierce conversation" is to:
▶ interrogate reality
▶ provoke learning
▶ tackle tough challenges
▶ enrich relationships.

It is about creating what Csikszentmihalyi (1993) has identified as a "moral code" and which Harris (2007) has refined into a values framework, which should include:
▶ respect—for self and others
▶ integrity—being true to self and others
▶ responsibility—to self and others
▶ cooperation—awareness and appreciation of others
▶ patience—with self, others and events
▶ beneficence—desire to promote well-being in others.

Of the many themes on leadership and management that are out there, the decision to select just four for this chapter was done on the basis that these alone seem to represent the crux of some of the issues facing so many schools today. Creating a culture of sharing and developing, of creating methods for decision-making, and supporting the development of a learning organization by paying attention to the emotional development of leaders, teachers and students is a very real 21st-century challenge.

Key questions

To what extent am I/is my school developing a positive culture that encourages student progress and the creation of a "moving school"?

Is my school developing as a "learning organization"?

Does my school pay sufficient attention to the importance of emotional intelligence and emotional leadership?

Leadership and change in the 21st century can perhaps be most aptly summarized by a 19th-century poet, Tennyson, in *In Memoriam*:

> *The hills are shadows, and they flow*
> *From form to form, and nothing stands;*
> *They melt like mist, the solid lands,*
> *Like clouds they shape themselves and go.*

Leaders and schools who recognize this will be closer to grasping the challenges of leadership and change than many others.

CHAPTER 9

In summary: meeting 21st-century learning challenges

Regardless of who you are or what you have been,
you can be what you want to be.

(Hill and Clement Stone 1981)

Our aim has been to add further stimulus to discussion about the many issues we face as educators in the ever-changing world of the 21st century. As Greenspan (2000) says:

Workers must be equipped not simply with technical know-
how but also with the ability to create, analyze and transform
information and to interact effectively with others. Moreover, that
learning will increasingly be a life-long activity.

As educators, we need to help in the preparation of our young people for the changing employment opportunities they will face, but our role is more than that as we seek to aid the holistic development of students, working with parents, families and the wider community. An awareness of our students' learning preferences, their digital world and brain dominances, together with an extension of our knowledge of emotional intelligences, motivation and thinking skills, will, we believe, help teachers and students grow their learning together.

We have not inherited this world from our parents. We have been
loaned it by our children.

Native American tradition

This world "loaned by our children" is clearly one of exponential change, whereby new technology is reshaping the global economy and previous world structures. Our children are growing up in an educational world in which the key concepts of effective communication, problem-solving, team-building and collaborative working are the lifelong learning skills that we must continue to encourage. To not only cope with the pace of change but to lead and enhance its global uniting possibilities, our young people must be increasingly aware of the innate skills of learning that can be engaged and further developed. In our technology- and knowledge-aware societies the real values of care, concern, self-respect and compassion remain key to human and social development. Self-awareness and self-esteem can only help us all learn to make a more valuable contribution locally, nationally and internationally as we all develop our learning skills.

Diana Laurillard (2007) notes:

> *Over the last hundred years or so, learning theorists such as Dewey, Piaget, Vygotsky, Bruner, Freire, Pask, Winogard, Papet, Resnick, Seely Brown, Marton, Biggs and Lare have expressed the nature of active learning in a variety of ways, from construction, to discovery learning, to meta-cognition, to situated learning ... but they all have in common the focus on the learner as being the active participant in the process.*

This common process seems to be gaining in relevance as we strive to direct, engage and instil a love of enquiry and curiosity in our digital-age students. Students need to interact with each other—those close and those distant—and, by doing so, knowledge becomes a social construct rather than a series of isolated facts passed from one individual to another.

Therefore, the 21st-century learners' self-awareness and lifelong learning skills can be developed through the following strategies.

Strategies

Relevance: students are engaged on real goal-oriented tasks rather than theoretical exercises.

Enquiry: students are engaged through exploring and experimenting and following natural curiosity.

Reinforcement: learning is reinforced through the practising of skills and using formative assessment and feedback.

Reflection: the opportunity to take time out—to interrogate and embed the learning processes, to think about learning (too often missing from our busy lives).

Articulation: talking about learning, explaining to others, showing self-awareness and understanding.

Creativity: exploring concepts, skills and knowledge from different angles, to explore and reconstruct in new ways.

To establish processes and opportunities the active learner requires different approaches by the teacher: a shift away from transmission models to the use of strategies that involve the learner in the process. This paradigm shift to more personalized learning activities can be supported by e-learning: making full use of the digital world's opportunities for collaboration, interaction, engagement, presentation and communication in an adaptive and engaging context.

A well-known author wrote of the need for a revolution in learning, with the aim of achieving "less din, less repetition and less unnecessary effort in schools" and a learning environment that is centred on the learner's own actions and focused on uncovering knowledge through enquiry rather than the repetition of test questions. The author was Jan Amos Komensky—better known as Comenius—and this statement was written more than 350 years ago. He also believed in a global education, drawing on the richness of human culture across national boundaries and aiming to improve the human condition, creating understanding and peace.

As the IB aims to develop "inquiring, knowledgeable and caring young people who help to create a better and more peaceful world through intercultural understanding and respect" (thus echoing the sentiments of Comenius), so an awareness of the development of our understanding of learning must support that aim. It is through finding the links in the world in which we live that true global learners can be developed. The increasing technological revolution of the 21st century is shrinking our world, enabling instant connectivity and supporting the sharing of educational principles across continents and cultures. With over 1 billion computers in the world and 1 billion mobile phones sold in a 12-month period, there is growing capacity to link our learners across the world, thus increasing knowledge and firing inquiry and understanding.

Building a greater understanding of the learning and cultures of other nations should lead to a greater understanding of the learning processes of the students in our own care. A raised awareness of the context of change allied to an increased understanding of the advances in neuroscience is building an increasing body of knowledge about the importance of the brain in the learning process. An awareness of how memory can be enhanced, how hemispherical preferences affect learning strategies and differences in male and female brain functions can offer opportunities for educators to reassess a range of learning approaches.

Building on brain-based approaches, we can explore the concepts of multi-sensory learning preferences and the significances of Gardner's Multiple Intelligences. Opening our minds to these aspects and avoiding the labelling of learners can enable us to engage with a more personalized approach to learning, focusing on student engagement, self-awareness and a multi-sensory learning system.

Increased awareness of brain-based and multi-sensory learning can link to adopting a thinking skills approach, whereby students and teachers are encouraged to grasp the concept of metacognition. An awareness of the thinking and learning process is a key lifelong learning skill that enables students to transfer their thinking and research skills from one area to another. Thinking skills also underpin questioning and inquiry and are a central aspect of the creative process.

Reflection

Does your school create time for students and teachers to explore the links between a range of learning strategies?

How does learning differ in your school from when you were a student?

How has technology impacted on your students' lives (a) in school and (b) at home?

Is there an openness of mind in the school to challenge assumptions about the learning process?

What are the barriers to a true 21st-century learning process? How might they be overcome?

The IB learner profile refers to the need for schools "to evaluate critically their learning environment", to bring about changes that "lead to a truly collaborative learning environment" and "to invest in professional development".

The aim of our book has been to contribute in some small way to that professional development by signposting some of the areas that warrant further exploration.

Klaus Seitz (2001) writes:

> The convergence of the world is driven by the economic imperative and education is trailing behind the globalization of business. As in the fable of the hare and the tortoise, education is always behind, is not setting the pace and is at best a corrective to social change ... what is needed above all is development of the ability to understand one another and to co-operate in a world beset by huge problems affecting the entire world, problems which can only be resolved through global partnerships.

The IB plays a key role in the development of that global partnership through the sharing of a central vision and creation of opportunities to share expertise and a passion for learning. Wherever our students reside—in different cultures and social settings—they each have personal learning needs. Each is a unique learning individual who is affected by aspects of brain hard-wiring, who has particular learning preferences and multiple intelligences and whose emotional intelligence and motivation are influenced by a complex interweaving of factors. Each has a unique role to play in our flattening, globalized world, and will require the lifelong learning skills of reflection, metacognition, inquiry, creativity, logical analysis, questioning, engagement, empathy, collaboration, confidence, reliability, perseverance and adaptability and, perhaps above all, an openness of mind to show understanding of others and acceptance of the need to be flexible while holding on to one's core human beliefs.

As Dryden and Vos (2001) wrote in their *Learning Revolution*,

> *We live at the most exciting of times where we can help shape the future for the better by helping our young people gain the vital lifelong learning skills they need to keep safe our world for their children.*

As educators, we too must accept the need to change.

> *Time change and higher human adaptation are not made by resistance to the old habits. Change is not a matter of **not** doing something; it is a matter of doing **something else**.*
>
> *Da Avabhasa*

As learners ourselves, we must exhibit the lifelong learning skills that we seek to develop in our students and, as long as we continue to face the increasing challenges of the pace of the 21st-century change with a true passion for learning, we can fulfil the bold aims of the IB. It does mean that we must have an open mind ourselves, and it is worth going back a thousand years from our current pace of life to reflect on these words taken from the tomb of a bishop buried in 1100 AD:

> *When I was young and free and imagination had no limits,*
> *I dreamed of changing the world.*
> *As I grew older and wiser,*
> *I discovered the world would not change,*
> *So I shortened my sights somewhat and decided*
> *To change only my country,*
> *But it seemed too immovable.*
> *As I grew into my twilight years*
> *In one last desperate attempt,*
> *I settled for changing my family,*
> *Those closest to me, but alas,*

They would have none of it.
And now as I lie on my death bed,
I suddenly realise:
If only I had changed myself,
Then by example I might have changed my family.
From their inspiration and encouragement
I would have been able to better my country, and who knows,
I may have changed the world.

In this world of global economic change, business may well be the hare and education the tortoise—but we know who eventually wins that race. By continuing to develop and share our passion for lifelong learning and by exhibiting the motivation for analysis, enquiry and creativity ourselves, we can by example lead our students forward into the most exciting time in the history of education. In a world of real-time global communication and increasing understanding of the learning processes we have the opportunity to help build a more relevant, coherent and better world of learning for all our young people.

The last 30 years have seen an explosion in the publication of books on the theories of management and leadership, assessment, curriculum, the management of pupil behaviour, schools of the future, technology, organizational structure, culture and other issues such as performance management. These can be seen as an embarrassment of riches or a nightmare. They do, however, reflect the massive debate surrounding education and the lack of agreement about what exactly is needed. Fifty years ago the UK had a consensus about the structure of education and about what should be taught in schools. This has broken down to such an extent that there has been little real consensus now for many years despite the very considerable sum of money that has been spent on education reform. This scenario is also true of many other countries, as Fullan, Hill and Crevola (2006) point out in their book *Breakthrough*:

> *Billions of dollars have been spent on education reform in the*
> *past decade and a half with results in literacy and maths, at best,*
> *inching forward. This is not value for money, nor is it satisfactory*
> *work for teachers, principals, students and parents.*

We need to get education and its management right, as Rischard (2002) states in *High Noon*:

> *The new world economy, with its knowledge intensity, requires*
> *a leap forward in each country's education effort—from primary*
> *to higher education, and even to lifelong learning and the*
> *accreditation of competencies.*

Schools face enormous challenges in the 21st century, not only in how children are taught, but also in what they are taught, the degree of involvement they have in the assessment process, how staff are managed, how much is invested in their training and indeed what focus that training has.

Ultimately, we will all depend on the next generation of students continuing to be enthusiastic about their learning and, above all, increasing the range of skills and competencies they posses to inform their individual needs, to understand and contribute to their local community and to help tackle the problems posed by globalization.

As educationalists we need to continually challenge our assumptions of the learning process, grow our own learning and model the attitudes of energy, openness, creative inquiry, flexibility and love of learning if we are to develop such attributes in our students.

This is the time of the greatest ever global change, providing increasing opportunities for our young people, and as learners and teachers we can play a significant role in developing the lifelong learning skills for the future.

A key aspect of our development of learning for the future will be the unlocking of creativity in our teachers and learners.

As Sir Ken Robinson (2001) says at the end of his excellent book *Out of Our Minds*:

> *Our own times are being swept along on an avalanche of innovations in science, technology, and social thought. To keep pace with these changes, or to get ahead of them, we will need all our wits about us—literally we must learn to be creative.*

Through our learning, creativity and energy we can "encourage students across the world to become active, compassionate and lifelong learners".

REFERENCES

Adey, P. and Shayer, M. 1994. *Really Raising Standards: Cognitive Intervention and Academic Achievement*. Oxford, UK. Routledge.

Bandura, A. 1986. *Social Foundations of Thought and Action: A Social Cognitive Theory*. New Jersey, USA. Prentice Hall.

Bellanca, J. 1997. *Active Learning Handbook*. Thousand Oaks, California. Corwin Press.

Birren, F. 1979. *Color Psychology and Color Therapy*. New York, New York. Citadel Press.

Black, P. and Wiliam, D. 1998. *Inside the Black Box*. London, UK. King's College.

Boyatzis, R. 1992. *The Competent Manager: A Model for Effective Performance*. New York, New York. John Wiley and Sons.

Boyatzis, R. 1994. "Stimulating Self Directed Learning through the Managerial Assessment and Development Course". *Journal of Management Education*. Vol 18. Pp 304–323.

Bracy, G. 2004. "The condition of public education: The 14th Bracy report", *Phi Delta Kappan* Vol 86. Pp 149–166.

Branden, N. 1994. *The Six Pillars of Self Esteem*. New York, New York. Bantam Press.

Bridgeland, J., DiIulio, J., Morison, K. 2006. *The Silent Epidemic: Perpectives of High School Dropouts*. New York, New York. Bill and Melinda Gates Foundation.

Brizendine, L. 2007. *The Female Brain*. New York, New York. Bantam Press.

Bryan, L. L. and Joyce, I. J. 2007. "Better strategy through organisation design." *The Mckinsey Quarterly* Vol 2. Pp 22–29.

Bush, T. and Bell, L. 2002. *The Principles and Practice of Educational Management*. London, UK. Paul Chapman Publishing.

Caldwell, J. 2006. *Exhilarating Leadership*. London, UK. Specialist Schools and Academies Trust.

Caruso, D. and Salovey, P. 2004. *The Emotionally Intelligent Manager*. San Francisco, CA. Jossey-Bass Publishing.

Caviglioli, O., Harris, I. and Tindall, B. 2002. *Thinking Skills and Eye Cue*. London, UK. Network Educational Press.

Combes, A. W., Miser A. B., Whitaker, K. S. 1999. *On Becoming a School Leader: A Person-Centered Challenge*. Alexandria, Virginia. Association for Supervision and Curriculum Development.

Costa, A. 2003. "The Thought-Filled Curriculum". In Williams, S. (ed.), *Teaching Thinking*. Birmingham, UK. Imaginative Minds Publishing.

Csikszentmihalyi, M. 1993. *The Evolving Self: A Psychology for the New Millennium.* New York, New York. Harper Perennial.

Davies, B. 2007. *Developing Sustainable Leadership.* London, UK. Paul Chapman Publishing.

Davies, B. and Ellison, L. 1997. *School Leadership for the 21st Century.* London, UK. Routledge.

de Bono, E. 1999. *Six Thinking Hats.* London. Penguin.

Deal, T. E. and Kennedy, A. 1983. "Culture and School Performance". *Educational Leadership.* Vol 40. Pp 140–141.

Dewey, J. 1910. *How we think.* London, UK. Cosimo Classics.

Dewey, J. 1916. *Democracy and Education: An Introduction to the Philosophy of Education.* New York, New York, Macmillan.

Dryden, G. and Vos, J. 2001. *The Learning Revolution.* London, UK. Network Educational Press Ltd.

Dufour, R. and Eaker, R. 1998. *Professional Learning Communities at Work: Best Practices for Enhancing Student Achievement.* Bloomington, Indiana. National Education Services.

Dunn, R. and Dunn, K. 1978. *Teaching Students through their Individual Learning Styles.* Upper Saddle River, New Jersey. Allyn and Bacon.

Edelman, G. M. 2007. *Second Nature: Brain Science and Human Knowledge.* New Haven, Connecticut. Yale University Press.

Everard, K., Morris, G. and Wilson, I. 2004. *Effective School Management.* London, UK. Paul Chapman Publishing.

Felder, R. and Silverman, L. 2005. "Learning and teaching styles in engineering education". *Engineering Education.* Vol 78. Pp. 674–681.

Fielding, R. 2005. "Learning, lighting and color: lighting design for schools and universities in the 21st century". *Professional Lighting Design.* Vol 45.

Fink, D. 2005. *Leadership for Mortals.* London, UK. Paul Chapman Publishing. (Also including workbook, 2006.)

Fogarty, R. 1997. *Brain Compatible Classrooms.* Skylight Professional Development.

Fogarty, R. and Opeka, K. 1988. *Start Them Thinking.* Thousand Oaks, California. Corwin Press.

Freitas, Sara de and Yapp, C. 2005. *Personalizing Learning in the 21st Century.* London, UK. Network Educational Press.

Friedman, T. L. 2005. *The World is Flat.* New York, New York. Farrar, Straus and Giroux.

Fullan, M. 2001. *The New Meaning of Education Change.* London, UK. RoutledgeFalmer.

Fullan, M. 2004. *Leading a Culture of Change. Personal Action Guide and Workbook.* San Francisco, California. Jossey-Bass.

Fullan, M. 2005. *Education in Motion, Leading in a Culture of Change.* UK and Ireland workshop tour.

Fullan, M. and Hargreaves, A. 1992. *What's Worth Fighting for in Your School?,* Berkshire, UK. Open University Press.

Fullan, M., Hill, P. and Crevola, C. 2006. *Breakthrough.* London, UK. Sage Publications Ltd.

Gardner, H. 1993. *Multiple Intelligences: The Theory in Practice.* New York, New York. Basic Books.

Gardner, H. and Hatch, T. 1989. "Multiple Intelligences Go to School". *Educational Researcher.* Vol 18. Pp. 4–10.

Garrett, B. 1987. *The Learning Organisation.* Glasgow, UK. William Collins.

Goldberg, E. 2006. *The Wisdom Paradox.* New York, New York. Gotham Books.

Goleman, D. 1996. *Emotional Intelligence.* London, UK. Bloomsbury Publishing.

Goleman, D. 1998. *Working with Emotional Intelligence.* London, UK. Bloomsbury Publishing.

Goleman, D. 2004. *Emotional Intelligence and Working with Emotional Intelligence.* London, UK. Bloomsbury Publishing.

Goleman, D. 2006. *Social Intelligence.* London, UK. Hutchinson.

Goleman, D., Boyatzis, R. and McKee, A. 2002. *The New Leaders.* London, UK. Time Warner Books UK.

Goleman, D., Boyatzis, R. and McKee, A. 2003. *Primal Leadership: Learning to Lead with Emotional Intelligence.* San Francisco, California. Jossey-Bass.

Greenfield, S. 1997. *The Human Brain: A Guided Tour.* New York, New York. Weidenfeld & Nicolson.

Greenspan, A. 2000. Speech at Journal of Financial Services Research and the American Enterprise Institute Conference. Washington DC, April 14. Available online: http: //www.federalreserve.gov/BoardDocs/Speeches/2000/20000414.htm.

Handy, C. B. 1998. *The Hungry Spirit: Beyond Capitalism—A quest for purpose in the Modern World.* New York, New York. Broadway Books.

Hargreaves, A. 1994. *Changing Teachers, Changing Times: Teachers, Work and Culture in the Postmodern Age.* London, UK. Cassell.

Hargreaves, A. 2001. "Emotional geographies of teaching". *The Teachers College Record.* Vol 103. Pp. 1056–1080.

Hargreaves, A. 2005. "Sustainable Leadership". In Davies, B. (ed.) *The Essentials of School Leadership.* London, UK. Paul Chapman Publishing.

Hargreaves, D. 2004. "Personalising learning—Aspirant Headteacher Programme". Presentation to the Specialist Schools Trust, 14–15 October.

Hargreaves, A. and Fink, D. 2006. *Sustainable Leadership.* San Francisco, California. Jossey-Bass.

Harris, B. 2007. *Supporting the Emotional Work of School Leaders.* London, UK: Paul Chapman Publishing.

Harris, A., Bennett, N. and Preedy, M. 1997. *Organizational Effectiveness and Improvement in Education.* Buckingham, UK. Open University Press.

Harris, A., Jamieson, I. and Russ, J. 1997. "A study of 'effective' departments in secondary schools". In Harris, A. *et al.* (eds) *Organisational Effectiveness and Improvement in Education.* Buckingham, UK. Open University Press.

Hartle, F. and Hobby, R. 2003. "Leadership in a Learning Community: your job will never be the same again". In Davies, B. and West Burham, J. (eds) *2003 Handbook of Educational Leadership.* London, UK: Pearson Longman.

Hill, N. and Clement Stone, W. 1981. *Success Through a Positive Mental Attitude.* New York, New York. Pocket Books.

Hirsch, E. D. Jr (ed.) 2007. *The Knowledge Deficit: Closing the Shocking Education Gap for American Children*. Boston, Massachusetts. Houghton Mifflin.

Hoffer, E. 1942. *The True Believer*. New York, New York. Harper Collins.

Hollwich, F. 1979. *The Influence of Ocular Light Perception on Metabolism in Man and in Animal*. New York, New York. Springer-Verlag.

Holmes, O. W. 1858. *The Autocrat of the Breakfast Table*. Boston Atlantic Monthly.

Honey, P. and Mumford, A. 1986. *Manual of Learning Styles*. Maidenhead, UK. Peter Honey Publications.

Hood, D. 2006. "Personalising learning through learning styles". In: Prashnig, B. *Learning Styles in Action*. London, UK. Network Continuum Press.

Hyerle, D. (ed.). 2004. *Student Successes with Thinking Maps*. Thousand Oaks, California. Corwin Press.

Jensen, E. and Johnson, G. 1995. *The Learning Brain*. Thousand Oaks, California. Brain Store Inc.

Johnson, S. 2006. *Everything Bad is Good for You*. Harmondsworth, UK. Penguin.

Kolb, D. 1984. *Experiential Learning*. Upper Saddle River, New Jersey. Prentice Hall.

Kolb, D. 2005. *The Kolb Learning Style Inventory*. Experience-Based Learning Systems, Inc.

Lake, M. and Needham, M. 1995. *Top Ten Thinking Tactics*. Birmingham, UK. Imaginative Minds.

Laurillard, D. 2007. "Technology in the service of our educational ambitions: bringing it into the mainstream". Keynote speech at the 12th Cambridge International Conference on Open and Distance Learning, September 2007.

Lazear, D. 2001. *Pathways of Learning: Teaching Students and Parents about Multiple Intelligences*. Albuquerque, New Mexico. University of New Mexico Press.

Lazear, D. 2002. *Eight Ways of Teaching*. Thousand Oaks, California. Corwin Press.

Lewis, C. 2004. "Building community in school: the child development project". In Elias, M. J., Arnold, H. and Hussy, C. S. (eds) *EQ + IQ = Best Leadership Practices for Caring and Successful Schools*. Thousand Oaks, California. Corwin Press.

Lipman, M. 2003. *Thinking in Education*. Cambridge, UK. Cambridge University Press.

Louis, K. and Kruse, S. (eds) 1995. *Professionalism and Community*. Thousand Oaks, California. Corwin Press.

Maslow, A. and Frager, R. 1954. *Motivation and Personality*. New York, New York. Harper.

McGregor, D. 2007. *Developing Thinking, Developing Learning*. Maidenhead, UK. Open University Press.

Newman, F. and Wehlage, G. 1995. *Successful School Restructuring*. Madison, Wisconsin. Center on Organisation and Restructuring of Schools.

November, A. 2001. *Empowering Students with Technology*. Thousand Oaks, California. Corwin Press.

Papert, S. 1996. *The Connected Family: Bridging the Digital Generation Gap*. Atlanta, Georgia. Longstreet Press.

Peters, T. J. and Waterman, R. H. 1995. *In Search of Excellence.* New York, New York. Harper and Row.

Pink, D. H. 2005. *A Whole New Mind.* Harmondsworth, UK. Penguin.

Pinker, S. 1997. *How the Mind Works.* Harmondsworth, UK. Penguin.

Polster, E. and Polster, M. 1974. *Gestalt Therapy Integrated.* New York, New York. Random House.

Prashnig, B. 1998. *The Power of Diversity.* Auckland, New Zealand. David Bateman Ltd.

Prashnig, B. 2006. *Learning Styles in Action.* London, UK. Network Continuum Press.

Preedy, M., Glatter, R. and Wise, C. 2003. *Strategic Leadership and Educational Improvement.* London, UK. Paul Chapman Publishing.

Prensky, M. 2001. *Digital Game Based Learning.* New York, New York. McGraw Hill.

Prensky, M. 2006. *Don't Bother Me Mom, I'm Learning.* New York. Paragon House.

Ratey, J. 2003. *A User's Guide to the Brain.* Auckland, New Zealand. Abacus Books.

Reich, R. 1992. *Work of Nations,* New York, New York. Vintage Press.

Restak, R. 2003. *The New Brain.* New York, New York. Rodale Books.

Restak, R. 2006. *The Naked Brain.* New York, New York. Harmony Books.

Riding, R. and Rayner, S. 1998. *Cognitive Styles and Learning Strategies.* London, UK. David Fulton.

Rischard, J. F. 2002. *High Noon.* New York, New York. Basic Books.

Robinson, K. 2001. *Out of Our Minds.* Mankato, Minnesota. Capstone Press.

Rockett, M. and Percival, S. 2002. *Thinking for Learning.* London, UK. Network Educational Press Ltd.

Rosenholtz, S. J. 1989. *Teachers' Workplace: The Social Organisation of Schools.* New York, New York. Longman.

Rowe, M. B. 1986. "Wait-time: slowing down may be a way of speeding-up!". *Journal of Teacher Education.* Vol 37. January–February. Pp. 43–50.

Sadler, D. R. 1989. "Formative assessment in the design of instructional systems". *Instructional Science.* Vol 18. Pp. 119–144.

Schilling D. 1996. *50 Activities for Teaching Emotional Intelligence.* Spring Valley, California. Interchoice Publishing.

Schwartz, B. 2004. *The Paradox of Choice.* London, UK. Harper Perennial.

Scott, S. 2004. *Fierce Conversations: Achieving Success at Work and in Life, One Conversation at a Time.* New York, New York. Berkley Publishing.

Seitz, K. 2001. "Global learning—challenges for education in school and outside school". *Adult Education and Development.* Vol 57.

Seligman, M. 1991. *Learned Optimism.* New York, New York. Knopf.

Senge, P. 2000. *Schools That Learn.* London, UK. Nicholas Brealy Publishing.

Sinofsky, E. R. and Knirck, F. G. 1981. "Choose the right color for your learning style". *Instructional Innovator.* Vol 26. Pp. 17–19.

Smith, A. 2002. *The Brain's Behind It.* London, UK. Network Educational Press Ltd.

Stoll, L. 1999. "School culture: black hole or fertile garden for school improvement". In: Prosser, J. (ed.) *School Culture*. London, UK. Paul Chapman Publishing.

Stoll, L. and Fink, D. 1996. *Changing Our Schools*. Buckingham, UK. Open University Press.

Stoll, L., Fink, D. and Earl, L. 2003. *It's About Learning: It's About Time*. London, UK. RoutlegeFalmer.

Swartz, R. J. 1995. *Infusing the Teaching of Critical and Creative Thinking into Content Instruction: A Lesson Design Handbook*. Mahwah, New Jersey. Lawrence Erlbaum.

Sylwester, R. 1995. *A Celebration of Neurons*. New York, New York. Association for Supervision and Curriculum Development.

Tice, L. 1997. *Personal Coaching for Results*. London, UK. Thomas Nelson Publishers.

Toffler, A. 1970. *Future Shock*. New York, New York. Random House.

Watson, L. 2007. "Building the future of learning". *European Journal of Education*. Vol 42. Pp. 255–263.

Winston, R. 2003. *The Human Mind*. New York, New York. Bantam Press.

Wiseman, R. 2003. *The Luck Factor*. New York, New York. Century Books.

APPENDIX

IB learner profile

The aim of all IB programmes is to develop internationally minded people who, recognizing their common humanity and shared guardianship of the planet, help to create a better and more peaceful world.

IB learners strive to be:

Inquirers	They develop their natural curiosity. They acquire the skills necessary to conduct inquiry and research and show independence in learning. They actively enjoy learning and this love of learning will be sustained throughout their lives.
Knowledgeable	They explore concepts, ideas and issues that have local and global significance. In so doing, they acquire in-depth knowledge and develop understanding across a broad and balanced range of disciplines.
Thinkers	They exercise initiative in applying thinking skills critically and creatively to recognize and approach complex problems, and make reasoned, ethical decisions.
Communicators	They understand and express ideas and information confidently and creatively in more than one language and in a variety of modes of communication. They work effectively and willingly in collaboration with others.
Principled	They act with integrity and honesty, with a strong sense of fairness, justice and respect for the dignity of the individual, groups and communities. They take responsibility for their own actions and the consequences that accompany them.
Open-minded	They understand and appreciate their own cultures and personal histories, and are open to the perspectives, values and traditions of other individuals and communities. They are accustomed to seeking and evaluating a range of points of view, and are willing to grow from the experience.

Caring	They show empathy, compassion and respect towards the needs and feelings of others. They have a personal commitment to service, and act to make a positive difference to the lives of others and to the environment.
Risk takers	They approach unfamiliar situations and uncertainty with courage and forethought, and have the independence of spirit to explore new roles, ideas and strategies. They are brave and articulate in defending their beliefs.
Balanced	They understand the importance of intellectual, physical and emotional balance to achieve personal well-being for themselves and others.
Reflective	They give thoughtful consideration to their own learning and experience. They are able to assess and understand their strengths and limitations in order to support their learning and personal development.

Index

NOTE: Page numbers in *italic figures* refer to figures.

T

target-setting 105
technological change
    exploring perceptions of 6–9
    instant connectivity 133
technology *see* information and
    communication technology
testing, standardized 102
theory of knowledge (TOK) 51
thinking
    creative and critical 48, 49, 52–3
    "imaginal thought" 53
    learning by 124
    parallel thinking 56
    phases of 52
    "propositioned thought" 53
    thinking cycle 57
    thinking for learning 53–5, *54*, 57
    thinking for learning strategies 58–68
    thinking skills 48, 52, *54*, 134
    see also cognitive processing;
    creative thinking; critical thinking;
    metacognition
thinking maps 62, *63*
"Three stars and a wish" strategy 104
Tice, Lou 81
timelines, conceptualizing
    history 13–14
Toffler, A. 10
TOK *see* theory of knowledge
triune brain theory 19
Turkey, visual arts students' visit 90–1
21st century living and learning 5–16

U

United Kingdom, curriculum
    provision 102–3
United States, narrowing of
    curriculum 102

V

VAK *see* Visual, auditory, kinaesthetic
    (VAK)
Venn diagrams ·108, *111*
verbal/linguistic intelligence 41, *44*
Versailles, Treaty of 15
Vidyalankar Institute of Technology 93
visual arts, student group in
    Turkey 90–1
visual, auditory, kinaesthetic
    (VAK) 36–42, *37*
    MI and VAK in a classroom *44*
    and learning preferences 45–6
visual learning style 40
    see also Visual, auditory, kinaesthetic
    (VAK)
visual/spatial intelligence 42, *44*
Vos, J. 5, 135
Vygotsky, Lev 48

W

"wait time", after asking a question 105
wall charts, history studies 13
Waterman, R. H. 113
"What Makes Good" strategy 104
whiteboards 22
"whole-brain" learning, strategies 24–5
whole-school approaches
    engaging meaningfully with
    students 108
    learning environment 99–100
William, Dylan 101, 109
Wiseman, Professor Richard 26–7
Wolff, Marie 69
women and men, differing brain
    structure 23
Woods, P. 69
word smart 42, *44*
workforce, required competencies 70
World Wide Web, pace of change 7, 8